EDITED BY **JO FACER**
SERIES EDITOR **TOM BENNETT**

THE research ED GUIDE TO

PROFESSIONAL DEVELOPMENT

....

AN EVIDENCE-INFORMED
GUIDE FOR TEACHERS

JOHN CATT
FROM HODDER EDUCATION

To order, please visit www.johncatt.com or contact Customer Service at education@hachette.co.uk / +44 (0)1235 827827.

ISBN: 978 1 0360 06433 3

© John Catt Educational Limited 2024

First published in 2024 by
John Catt from Hodder Education,
An Hachette UK Company
15 Riduna Park, Station Road,
Melton, Woodbridge IP12 1QT
www.johncatt.com

Typeset in the UK.

Printed in the UK.

A catalogue record for this title is available from the British Library.

MIX
Paper | Supporting
responsible forestry
FSC
www.fsc.org
FSC™ C104740

WHAT IS researchED?

researchED is an international, grassroots education-improvement movement that was founded in 2013 by Tom Bennett, a London-based high school teacher and author. researchED is a truly unique, teacher-led phenomenon, bringing people from all areas of education together on to a level playing field. Speakers include teachers, principals, professors, researchers and policymakers.

Since our first sell-out event, researchED has spread all across the UK, into the Netherlands, Norway, Sweden, Australia and the US, with events planned in Spain, Japan, South Africa and more. We hold general days as well as themed events, such as researchED Maths & Science, or researchED Tech.

WHO ARE WE?

Since 2013, researchED has grown from a tweet into an international conference movement that so far has spanned six continents and 13 countries. We have simple aims: to help teaching become more evidence-facing; to raise the research literacy in teaching; to improve education research standards; and to bring research users and research creators closer together. To do this, we hold unique one-day conferences that gather together teachers, researchers, academics and anyone touched by research. We believe in teacher voice, and short-circuiting the top-down approach to education that benefits no one.

HOW DOES IT WORK?

The gathering of mainly teachers, researchers, school leaders, policymakers and edu-bloggers creates a unique dynamic. Teachers and researchers can attend the sessions all day and engage with each other to exchange ideas. The vast majority of speakers stay for the duration of the conference, visit each other's sessions, work on the expansion of their knowledge and gain a deeper understanding of the work of their peers. Teachers can take note of recent developments in educational research, but are also given the opportunity to provide feedback on the applicability of research or practical obstacles.

CONTENTS

FOREWORD
TOM BENNETT

This is a book about professional development. But in some ways, it is not a book about professional development. Because for the first claim to be entirely true we would have to be talking about a profession, and in some ways, teaching is not a profession at all. Because for a field to be a profession it has to have a shared body of agreed professional domain knowledge and skills. It would need to be bound by a shared ethos and moral code. Neither of which teaching can be said to enjoy.

We can barely agree on the aims of education, let alone the aims of teaching. Views on pedagogy, curriculum, assessment, behaviour management and everything in between are disputed so fiercely that the sector can be characterised as a theatre of war as much as a community unified by principle and a shared, foundational knowledge.

Teacher training is sometimes a part of this muddle – teachers can leave feeling more confused and less capable than they did before, if the course itself is a muddied, ideological mess – but it is part of a broader problem within the ecosystem. In the UK, I led a national review of how behaviour was trained and found, to my complete unsurprise, that it was overall, not trained very much at all. The consensus appeared to be 'you'll pick this up as you go along.' Which is fine if you do, and terrible if you don't, and frequently, many teachers didn't. 'Working something out for yourself' isn't how you create professionals. You wouldn't train a plumber like that, let alone a doctor or an accountant. It is a process almost designed to do the exact opposite to building professional competence.

Things fare no better when it comes to professional understandings of how students learn, how memory works, how motivation, focus, comprehension are best understood; things that one might reasonably believe were fundamental to the practice of teaching.

But this is not the fault of teacher training alone – some of which, a significant minority perhaps, is still good, and often getting better. Institutions like schools have evolved over the decades, rather than with intention or guided by professional bodies who maintain its professional integrity (the professional bodies we do possess in the UK are often propelled as much by their own constituent ideologies and the need to sustain their own membership bases and revenue sources, as they are by achieving some kind of professional unity).

As a result, teachers have endured the vagaries and whims of faux professional development for decades. I have sat through sessions that asked attendees to tell jokes to one another, to draw posters of what their ideal 'teacher superhero' would look like, where we had to walk around a room saying nice things to one another, where we were exhorted to do things that had no evidence bases whatsoever, like Brain Gym and other forms of mysticism. Countless men and women sitting with their heads in their hands as they endured pointless, mindless CPD while trying not to weep.

As a result, what constitutes competence in teaching and leadership varies from shop to shop, depending on the varying ideologies and beliefs of the school governors, local authority panjandrums, or MAT leaders. The current UK teaching standards are noble, but so abstract as to be practically meaningless. No one in the field actually consults them at any time; they are like books buried in coffins with their owners, never again to be read in life.

But there is nothing false about hope, and there is hope. The last ten years have seen a massive renewal of the ambition to become a profession, a gathering sense of a burgeoning profession waiting to recreate itself. It has gone from a whisper in the wings, to a nervous cough, into a confident conversation, as across the world, teachers and leaders have woken up to the opportunities suggested by leaning into evidence-informed practice. We have seen an emergent confidence in our demi-profession because finally we have something to base our theories on other than intuition, instinct and superstition.

So we are now in the first phase of what I call the professionalisation of teaching. It will take years and years and thousands of bodies and conversations before we get there, but get there we can, and will.

And when we do get there, it will be because of books like this, and voices and minds like the ones Jo has assembled here in these pages. One day soon we can look back on the icebreakers, the learning styles, the star jumps, turning to our partners and telling them a surprising fact, and laugh. One day we will see professional development as a continuous and guaranteed entitlement, and wonder that we ever saw it as anything less than that. We will wave goodbye to pointless mandatory training that ticks boxes and serves no purpose.

And then we can call teaching a profession. And everyone wins.

Professor Tom Bennett, OBE
Founder of researchED

INTRODUCTION

JO FACER

It has long been acknowledged that the defining feature of great learning is a great teacher, and that, at scale, 'the quality of an education system cannot exceed the quality of its teachers' (Barber & Mourshed, 2007). While there are many routes to growing great schools, investing in the quality of the teachers who stand before children every day is one of the best bets to improve both pupils' educational outcomes and their experience of school.

Crucially, teacher quality is not fixed – all teachers can always improve. As the oft-quoted Dylan Wiliam says: 'Every teacher needs to improve, not because they are not good enough, but because they can be even better.' (Wiliam, 2012).

As you will find throughout this book, professional development influences, or should influence, every aspect of schools. It is not solely about the teaching techniques we use in the classroom, but encompasses the way we learn to think about the curriculum, how we manage behaviour, and even how we behave as leaders.

To open, Jon Hutchinson delves further into the importance of professional development, and makes the case for you spending a decent chunk of your precious time with this book. He ranges over the challenges of professional development, alongside the benefits to teachers, pupils and the education system as a whole, before sharing his recommendations for schools.

You will then hear from Elisabeth Bowling on whole school continuing professional development (CPD). She weighs up the balance between pre-planning a cycle of professional development and leaving flexibility to respond to emerging needs or school priorities; how to ensure cohesion between programmes for those at different stages of their careers, and how to implement these ideas successfully in a school.

Nimish Lad will next take us through the importance of practice in professional development, exploring what to practise and how, along with ways to ensure practice has impact in classrooms and schools.

Turning to new teachers next, Reuben Moore and a team of education researchers from the National Institute of Teaching share the best evidence and practice around how to develop colleagues at the very start of their teaching careers, both in terms of building domain expertise and embedding this in their practice.

Summer Turner then shares how schools might go about planning their annual CPD calendar, touching on aligning professional development to school priorities, considering how time might be used across an academic year, and what the right balance between all-staff facing and more bespoke CPD might be.

Building on this, Madeleine Fresko-Brown dives deeper into INSET days, the cornerstone of most teachers' professional development experiences, considering what makes these successful.

Hailing from one of the first trusts to systematise coaching for all members of staff, Jenny Thompson shares how her thinking has evolved over the years, and how coaching can distribute leadership, as well as how whole-school systems might support its impact.

We turn next to thinking about professional development in terms of how we develop leaders. Isaac Moore considers how we might go about identifying leadership development needs and responding to them, and what this could look like when embedded in a school context – including some of the softer skills like managing others and having challenging conversations.

Continuing the leadership thread, Adam Robbins explores how middle leaders might develop teaching in their departments, thinking about how to identify a focus, plan out priorities, structure professional development effectively and embed practices.

Finally, Jon Gilbert reflects on leading professional development across a trust, and how the role of a trust CPD lead might improve teacher practice at scale. He considers the various ways such an executive leader might support multiple schools.

All the writers in this book have longstanding experience and clear expertise in professional development, including time spent in schools walking the walk. They are trailblazers, carefully considering what we might learn from cutting-edge research, and how we might apply this to the messy, on-the-ground reality of schools today. I hope you will find in these chapters new innovations, as well as reassuring insights, that chime with your own beliefs and practices.

Ultimately, this book makes the case that for our schools to improve, we would be well advised to focus time, effort and energy in helping our teachers improve in all aspects of the role. Investing in professional development is both a genuine joy for individuals who joined a profession focused on learning, and an absolute necessity to create schools that deliver the experiences and outcomes for young people to surpass expectations, thrive emotionally and socially, and go on to live lives of limitless potential.

researchED guides

The researchED Guide to Professional Development complements the other books in the researchED series:

- *The researchED Guide to Educational Myths* (2019), edited by Craig Barton.
- *The researchED Guide to Explicit and Direct Instruction* (2019), edited by Adam Boxer.
- *The researchED Guide to Literacy* (2019), edited by James Murphy.
- *The researchED Guide to Assessment* (2020), edited by Sarah Donarski.
- *The researchED Guide to Leadership* (2020), edited by Stuart Lock.
- *The researchED Guide to The Curriculum* (2020), edited by Clare Sealy.
- *The researchED Guide to Special Educational Needs* (2021), edited by Karen Wespieser.
- *The researchED Guide to English as an Additional Language* (2022), edited by Hamish Chalmers.
- *The researchED Guide to Cognitive Science* (2023), edited by Kate Jones.
- *The researchED Guide to Primary Literacy* (forthcoming), edited by Stephen Lockyer.

References

Barber, M. & Mourshed, M. (2007). *How the World's Best-Performing School Systems Come Out on Top*, London and New York: McKinsey & Company.

Wiliam, D. (2012). SSAT Conference Keynote 2012 available at https://www.youtube.com/watch?v=r1LL9NX1hUw.

CHAPTER 1
MAKING THE CASE FOR PROFESSIONAL DEVELOPMENT
JON HUTCHINSON

Jon Hutchinson is Director of Curriculum and Professional Development at the Reach Foundation. He was a primary school teacher and assistant head, and has taught at Advanced and Masters Degree levels. Since 2022, Jon has held an international fellowship with New America on the Learning Sciences Exchange; he is also cofounder of the Meno Academy – a platform providing subject knowledge videos for primary school teachers. He holds a Masters in educational research from the University of Cambridge. Jon contributes to http://www.jonhutchinson.com and www.meno.academy and can be contacted on: jon.hutchinson@reachfoundation.org.uk.

Introduction

Making the case for continuing professional development (CPD) in teaching – as I'll attempt to do in this chapter – is a peculiar task, given that the alternative is *not* continuing to develop as a professional. Who could possibly be against it?

After all, Robinson (2011) demonstrated that of the five leadership domains that have a positive impact on pupil outcomes, 'promoting and participating in teacher learning and development' has the largest effect, double that of the nearest positive domains focused on setting goals and organising the curriculum.

Then there's Ingersoll and Strong (2011) who showed through a critical review of 15 empirical studies that strong professional development during induction to the profession results in 'improved teacher commitment and retention, teacher classroom instructional practices, and student achievement'. Finally, an evidence review and meta-analysis by Fletcher-Wood and Zuccollo (2020) found that professional development is a cost-effective way to improve pupil outcomes, with an overall effect size of 0.9. This is the equivalent of being taught by a teacher with ten years of experience.

So that's that, isn't it? CPD is a good idea and we should all do loads of it. Case closed.

Not so fast. Hiding just below the surface of each of these research findings is a huge caveat, one that any teacher who has sat through an INSET knows all too well: not all CPD is equal. Not by a long shot. In fact, the impact of CPD varies hugely on almost any measure that we might be interested in, including teacher effectiveness and pupil outcomes.

The research on professional development: a Tower of Babel

Part of this muddle comes from deep-rooted and long-standing philosophical differences in educational literature on teacher development. Coe (1999) pithily summarised the problem: 'One person's "effective practice" is another's 'neo-liberal hegemony'. In other words, while I might believe that a centrally planned curriculum is every teacher's entitlement that will increase coherence for pupils, a colleague may believe that it is an inexcusable affront to their professional autonomy and judgement, guaranteed to kill lessons and learning.

Zeichner (1983) identified at least four paradigms that collectively provide a 'matrix of beliefs and assumptions about the nature and purposes of schooling, teaching, teachers, and their education that gives shape to specific forms of practice in teacher education'. They are defined as follows:

1. **The craft paradigm**: this conceives of teaching as a vocation that is hard earned through trial and error, experience and apprenticeship, and the gradual accumulation of wisdom.

2. **The repertoire paradigm**: this emphasises the building and understanding of more comprehensive instructional modes, such as the direct-instruction approaches.

3. **The competency (or expert) paradigm**: this argues that underpinning teacher effectiveness is a body of knowledge and set of skills, empirically validated and gradually acquired through study and practice.

4. **The holistic or reflective paradigm**: this emphasises continual reflection from the teacher on the purposes of education, especially from a moral and political perspective, and how they are contributing to those goals.

We can see here, perhaps, a precursor to what we might today describe as the traditionalist–progressive paradigms. And we can imagine that what feels like meaningful professional development to teachers ascribing to either of those paradigms would be hell for the other group.

It's not just philosophical difficulties that plague education research related to professional development. There is also no agreed, underlying theory to the field, no standard model, no clear organising framework. This is usually taken as a key feature of a mature scientific field as without it, enquiry cannot be undertaken systematically and objectively.

This, in turn, leads to methodological differences that go beyond the usual positivist vs interpretivist debate. To bluntly characterise this difference, depending on the field of study and nature of the enquiries, it is usual for researchers to choose different approaches to collecting data and drawing conclusions. They may, for example, opt for quantitative data to 'prove' a hypothesis (positivism) or they may favour a more qualitative approach that allows for some interpretation in presenting conclusions (interpretivism).

However, educational researchers rarely get to even this point of disagreement, as they engage in fundamentally different claims about the field and, indeed, reality with no real edifice from which to assert validity. While doctors can at least agree that the goal is to make sick people better (and can therefore test whether medicines achieve this aim), teachers often disagree about the aims of education or even the definition of learning.

Finally, there is the challenge of actually measuring the things that you are interested in. Let's take the example of teacher effectiveness. Imagine that you are an educational researcher and are interested in this concept. How would you go about investigating whether or not a teacher is effective? One option is to give pupils tests when teachers first start teaching them, and then again after a year or so. Indeed, this is a common approach. Many internal performance-management systems in schools include a version of this 'measure progress' approach.

But we can immediately see a problem here. First, this sort of quantitative approach lends itself better to subjects that have largely right or wrong answers (such as mathematics or science). It is not as straightforward with many other subjects, such as English, where there is an element of subjectivity around quality. Even if we could design perfect pre- and post- tests (and that's a very big 'if'), how would we disentangle the progress that pupils would have made anyway from the progress that resulted from that particular teacher? And that's before we get into questions of the pupils' background characteristics, which we know have a huge influence on the variance of pupil achievement.

There are ways to mitigate each of these, including through the use of controls and sophisticated multi-level statistical analyses, but we can see that making claims about teacher effectiveness turns out to be rather complex, caveated and nuanced. If we were feeling gloomy, we might even say that it is impossible to make any meaningful claims with a degree of certainty beyond 'I reckon'.

Maybe we could just observe the teachers instead. Surely experienced leaders and educational researchers know good teaching when they see it? It turns out not. Teachers who have received a grade following a lesson observation have long been suspicious that the observer is really rating things like how much the lesson aligns to their own personal preferences or how well the pupils behaved (easier if you've got a top set, for example).

These suspicions were confirmed in a large study conducted on behalf of the Bill & Melinda Gates Foundation, called the Measures of Effective Teaching Project. The foundation has donated billions of dollars to education projects promising to develop teachers, and so the question of whether you can measure teacher effectiveness was by no means academic. After all, if you can't measure teacher effectiveness, how will you know whether you made any teachers any better? How can you know whether your billions are being wasted?

The results of the study were startling. Even when using what researchers call 'high inference observational instruments' (Kane et al., 2013), the chance of two independent observers giving a lesson the same grade was roughly half: the toss of a coin. If a lesson received the lowest grade from one observer, the inter-rater reliability of the observers dropped to 10%. This means that two independent observers watching the same lesson would only agree that it was inadequate one in ten times.

Other measures that might seem like good ideas also have significant issues. For example, asking pupils to rate their teachers' effectiveness would work hugely in your favour ... as long as you happened to be male. A neat study by MacNell, Driscoll and Hunt (2015) showed a significant gender bias resulting in teachers presented to online classes as male receiving much higher ratings than teachers presented as female.

These philosophical and methodological challenges may feel to many school leaders like navel gazing, best left to folks in education faculties and policy wonks who have the luxury of time to debate them. But if we hope to build high quality CPD for teachers, it is necessary to face them head on. In too many schools there is an illusion of consistency around purposes, principles and practices of effective teaching.

The first step for schools in providing effective professional development, then, is agreeing a set of shared principles, grounded in evidence and articulated clearly. At Reach Academy Feltham, my colleagues Matilda Browne and

Claire Couves have organised these into six broad domains: culture, planning, exposition, practice, assessment and feedback. Within each of these areas, 10 habits are set out. For example, within exposition one habit is: 'gradually fade guidance to promote the independence of pupils'. This is grounded in Sweller et al.'s (2019) cognitive load theory and takes into account the redundancy effect.[1]

Case for the defence: why investing in high-quality CPD is still worth it

There are three reasons why, despite the difficulties explored above, high-quality CPD is still worth the investment. If we get it right, it's good for teachers, it's good for pupils and it's good for the wider education sector. Let's take each in turn.

High-quality CPD is good for teachers

Everyone likes to feel as if they are getting better at stuff that they care about. There is immense satisfaction in feeling yourself improve. This deep motivational drive is often summarised in one of the three parts from Daniel Pink's (2011) popular 'mastery, autonomy, purpose' triumvirate. Pink argues that while we believe that people are primarily motivated by extrinsic rewards and sanctions, the truth is that what drives all people is a need to master what they are working on, and to have the autonomy to achieve the goal in a way that works for them and is clearly associated with their own goals. The reverse is also true. People become demotivated when they are not competent at something and cannot feel themselves getting any better at it. Similarly, having to follow strict protocols tends to demotivate people as they no longer feel as though they are in control of their own actions. Finally, very few people can muster energy or enthusiasm for work that they feel is pointless or lacks purpose.

Luckily, pretty much all teachers have the purpose criterion built in. They are driven by one, often moral, purpose, that of supporting their pupils to flourish. But the mastery part isn't a given in teaching. It's not uncommon for teachers to feel as though they aren't quite good enough. Even the most experienced teachers can walk out of a lesson feeling they have far from mastered their craft.

---

1   Cognitive load theory asserts that for information-processing purposes, the mind is made up of working memory (which is extremely limited and easily overloaded) and long-term memory (which is effectively limitless and organises information in schemas). The redundancy effect refers to the phenomenon of learners becoming 'cognitively overloaded' by receiving too much irrelevant information, such as large amounts of text on slides, or strict success criteria of familiar processes.

Many teachers, especially those who have been teaching for a few years, feel as though they are stagnating. And too many of those teachers then quit. On the other hand, when people feel as though they are improving at something that matters to them, they stick around. It's relatively rare for someone to quit at anything when they can clearly see themselves improving day by day and year by year.

High-quality CPD is good for the education system

As well as securing more positive outcomes for their pupils, then, teachers who benefit from high-quality CPD are more likely to enjoy their work, create a positive environment and stay in their school and the profession. A culture of low stakes, high support for teacher improvement has been shown to improve pupil results, but this sense of success also creates a positive effect on teacher retention (Kraft & Papay, 2014).

A profession that does not see a constant churn of teachers, but instead enjoys a more stable workforce with high levels of morale, is good for the education system more generally. Teachers are able to form longer-term relationships with colleagues and pupils, less money is poured down the drain of supply agencies, and schools don't feel like they are constantly starting back at square one each September. It is also, I would suggest more speculatively, likely to have a positive effect on recruitment, as teaching is viewed externally as a long-term and enjoyable career, potentially creating a virtuous cycle of prestige, pride and quality.

High-quality CPD is good for pupils

Perhaps most importantly, professional development can have a strong positive effect on pupil outcomes. Although a direct link is often tricky to isolate ('professional development' is a huge umbrella; there are many factors that contribute to pupil attainment), a review of 1300 studies (Yoon et al., 2007), whittled down to just nine that met the rigorous selection criteria, indicated that where teachers receive substantial professional development, they enjoy 21 percentile points of additional progress (as measured with a pre- and post- test).

A large randomised controlled trial[2] involving over 5000 primary school pupils found a similar amount of progress on maths attainment when using

---

2   Randomised controlled trials (or RCTs) are often considered the 'gold standard' of research as they try to prove the effectiveness of a treatment by allocating half the participants into the treatment while the other half receive 'business as usual'. If progress is made in the treatment group, researchers can be more confident that it was as a result of the treatment, as opposed to some other factor. In this example, the RCT was in fact 'four armed', with groups including: teachers using QTR led by a researcher; teachers using QTR led by a trainer; teachers using a standard peer-observation approach; and a group using only their usual approach to professional development.

a structured professional development approach known as quality teaching rounds (QTR) (Gore et al., 2021). Developed in the early 2000s, QTR is an approach involving peer observation grounded in a comprehensive model that includes 18 pedagogical elements. There are four stages to a QTR. First, a discussion based on a piece of professional reading takes place. Next, a full lesson by one member of the professional learning community (PLC) is observed. Then, the lesson is coded against the 18 elements (including items such as 'explicit quality criteria', 'deep knowledge' and 'inclusivity'). Finally, a group discussion is undertaken by all members of the PLC in which they share their coding and reach consensus on key themes.

Although academic outcomes feature much more widely as measures in the literature (indeed all of the studies in the aforementioned meta-analysis were focused on attainment in maths, reading, English and science), broader affective outcomes have also been shown to improve through high-quality professional development (Creemers & Kyriakides, 2010). But what exactly is 'high-quality' CPD? Happily, we've learned a lot in the last few years, thanks to rigorous research like the QTR trial, which shed light on the active ingredients of effective professional development. The final section in this chapter will set out what the evidence currently suggests are the best bets for improving pupil outcomes through professional development.

A way forward: towards a standard model for professional development in education

This chapter began with the rather pessimistic tableau of an ideologically divided field of research and, in turn, a teaching profession that cannot agree on fundamental constructs like teacher effectiveness or student outcomes. On the other hand, we have seen that there exists a huge prize of improved pupil progress, teacher effectiveness, job satisfaction and benefits to the broader educational system.

So, the question that faces us is: how do we go about achieving high-quality CPD given the difficulties explored above? The Education Endowment Foundation (EEF) was also interested in this question and, as a result, commissioned a systematic review and meta-analysis on the key characteristics of professional development (2021), which were associated with improvements in pupil achievement. A less technical guidance report (2021) was then produced, designed to allow school leaders and teachers to practically apply the findings. Rather than focusing on CPD as a general approach, or even specific programmes or forms of professional development, the EEF instead investigated the deeper, underpinning elements of effective approaches. These elements are referred to as 'mechanisms' and are grouped into four categories:

1. **Building knowledge**
   - Managing cognitive load
   - Revisiting prior learning

2. **Motivating teachers**
   - Setting and agreeing on goals
   - Presenting information from a credible source
   - Providing affirmation and reinforcement after progress

3. **Developing teaching techniques**
   - Instruction
   - Social support
   - Modelling
   - Monitoring and feedback
   - Rehearsal

4. **Embedding practice**
   - Providing prompts and cues
   - Prompting action planning
   - Encouraging monitoring
   - Prompting context-specific repetition

There are other notable models, such as Danielson's Framework for Teaching (2008) or Creemers and Kyriakides' Dynamic Approach to School Improvement (2010), the latter of which makes a compelling case for a theoretically unified and empirically validated approach to professional development (Antoniou & Kyriakides, 2013). However, these models lack, in my experience, an accessibility and user friendliness that is necessary for busy school leaders, where efficiency is often just as important as efficacy.

The 14 mechanisms of the EEF, on the other hand, are useful for both auditing criteria and as a planning tool. They caused me to reflect on my own botched experiences of planning CPD for teachers as an assistant head. Too often, my sessions were badly weighted toward just one group of mechanisms. I'm sure that on more than one occasion I spent the entire hour-long session focusing only on building knowledge, presenting fascinating findings from educational research and interrogating the underlying theories of how pupils learn. While this may have supported teachers in building their knowledge, there was little attempt to motivate teachers, develop some actionable techniques or embed any of it into practice.

On other occasions, I presented teaching strategies in what was essentially a 'tips and tricks' approach, such as showing teachers how they could 'silently model' in lessons (a pedagogical approach in which the teacher remains completely silent while demonstrating how to complete a task using only gestures and board-work). There was little discussion here of the social norms that were being capitalised on to focus pupil attention, or how cognitive load was carefully managed by limiting the flow of information that pupils were required to process in working memory. As a result, teachers might have given it a go, but the technique was ripe for misapplication, misinterpretation and lethal mutation.

It may be worth taking a moment to reflect on CPD that you have received, or perhaps even delivered, and benchmarking it against these groups of mechanisms. Were any areas missing? Did any dominate?

The aim with the mechanisms is not to shoehorn every single one into every professional development session, but rather to ensure that overall professional development sequences are well balanced, incorporating as many mechanisms as is appropriate and possible over time. An example, and how I wish I had planned and delivered professional development, might look like the following:

Focus	Formative assessment and adaptive teaching
Week 1	Pre-reading: EEF blog entitled Moving from 'differentiation' to 'adaptive teaching'
Week 2	Co-constructing success criteria for common strategies: check for understanding, show call, hinge questions, entry tickets
Week 3	Crafting effective multiple choice questions, key principles, models and practice
Week 4	Translating principles into practice using planning with subject/phase colleagues
Week 5	Rehearsal of planned adaptive-teaching techniques in triads
Week 6	Evaluation, bringing examples of pupil work and/or other artefacts

We can see that a key area has been selected – adaptive teaching – perhaps in response to a whole-school priority or as part of a systematic approach at developing the effective teaching principles agreed by teachers and leaders. We can see that the sequence begins by presenting evidence from a credible source: the EEF. This session might involve prompt questions such as 'What is the difference between differentiation and adaptive teaching, and why does it matter?'. Discussion in response to this promotes the activation of prior learning in the area, as well as peer collaboration.

Time is also given to set goals and ensure that teachers are involved in these, by co-constructing the success criteria for specific strategies. These techniques are thus developed and enhanced through social support as colleagues work together to define 'what good would look like', which effectively creates a model.

Opportunities are given for rehearsal and deliberate practice, where teachers can translate the principle into their own subject and in their own style. And finally, soft accountability is built in through an evaluation driven by each teacher, which should also allow for an indication of positive (or negative!) results, and give an opportunity for feedback.

Not all of the mechanisms are present, but over six weeks there is a balance of the four areas, meaning teachers get the chance to build their knowledge, develop techniques and feel motivated to adapt their teaching and embed the new knowledge into their practice. The process does not feel overwhelming to plan, deliver or participate in, and so high-quality CPD that is likely to result in improved pupil outcomes is achievable and desirable in the vast majority of schools.

Conclusion

To conclude, here are 10 recommendations that are grounded in a synthesis of the research presented in this chapter, coupled with my experience of working with hundreds of schools in building high-quality professional development.

Recommendation 1: Schools should clearly articulate a set of principles of effective teaching practice, as they understand them, informed by evidence. All professional-development activities should be grounded in, and consistent with, these principles.

Recommendation 2: Time should be prioritised and protected for professional-development activities, with leadership emphasising the potential to improve pupil outcomes.

Recommendation 3: Schools should provide a clear, cohesive CPD offer to teachers, indicating what is mandatory, what is encouraged and what is optional.

Recommendation 4: Schools should balance both knowledge-building and opportunities for practice during professional development.

Recommendation 5: Schools should sequence group-CPD activities coherently, with opportunities to revisit key ideas, iterate practice and deepen understanding of the underlying theory and principles.

Recommendation 6: Schools should provide individualised professional-development opportunities that address teachers' specific wants and needs.

Recommendation 7: Schools should ensure regular evaluation of professional development, perhaps led by teachers sharing 'artefacts' revealing the impact on pupil outcomes.

Recommendation 8: Professional development should be used to foster a sense of collegiality, high trust and mutual respect.

Recommendation 9: Time and trust should be given to teachers to translate principles into phase- and subject-specific approaches and strategies.

Recommendation 10: Schools should minimise workload issues associated with CPD by making use of resources and services from credible organisations such as the Chartered College of Teaching, the EEF, the National Institute of Teaching and, of course, researchED.

References

Antoniou, P. & Kyriakides, L. (2013). 'A Dynamic Integrated Approach to teacher professional development: Impact and sustainability of the effects on improving teacher behaviour and student outcomes'. *Teaching and Teacher Education*, 29(1), pp.1–12.

Coe, R. (1999). 'A manifesto for evidence-based education'. Centre for Evaluation and Monitoring.

Collin, J., & Smith, E. (2021). 'Effective Professional Development. *Guidance Report. Education Endowment Foundation (Crown Copyright)*.

Creemers, B.P. & Kyriakides, L. (2010). 'Using the Dynamic Model to develop an evidence-based and theory-driven approach to school improvement'. *Irish Educational Studies*, 29(1), pp.5–23.

Danielson, C. (2008). *The Handbook for Enhancing Professional Practice: Using the Framework for Teaching in Your School*. Alexandria, USA: ASCD.

EEF. (2021). 'Effective professional development: guidance report'. Education Endowment Foundation. Available at: https://educationendowmentfoundation. org.uk/education-evidence/guidance-reports/effective-professional-development.

Fletcher-Wood, H. & Zuccollo, J. (2020). 'The effects of high-quality professional development on teachers and students: A rapid review and meta-analysis'. Education Policy Institute and Wellcome Trust.

Gore, J.M., Miller, A., Fray, L., Harris, J. & Prieto, E. (2021). 'Improving student achievement through professional development: Results from a randomised controlled trial of Quality Teaching Rounds'. *Teaching and Teacher Education*, 101, 103297.

Ingersoll, R.M. & Strong, M.A. (2011). 'The impact of induction and mentoring programs for beginning teachers: A critical review of the research'. *Review of Educational Research*, 81(2), pp.201–233.

Kane, T.J., McCaffrey, D.F., Miller, T. & Staiger, D.O. (2013). 'Have we identified effective teachers?: Validating measures of effective teaching using random assignment (a research paper)'. MET Project. Bill & Melinda Gates Foundation. Available at: https://files.eric.ed.gov/fulltext/ED540959.pdf.

Kraft, M.A. & Papay J.P. (2014). 'Can professional environments in schools promote teacher development? Explaining heterogeneity in returns to teaching experience'. *Educational Evaluation and Policy Analysis*, 36(4), pp.476–500. doi:10.3102/0162373713519496.

MacNell, L., Driscoll, A. & Hunt, A.N. (2015). 'What's in a name: Exposing gender bias in student ratings of teaching'. *Innovative Higher Education*, 40, pp.291–303.

Pink, D.H. (2011). *Drive: The Surprising Truth about What Motivates Us*. Edinburgh: Canongate Books.

Robinson, V. (2011) *Student-centered Leadership* (Vol. 15). Hoboken, US: John Wiley & Sons.

Sims, S., Fletcher-Wood, H., O'Mara-Eves, A., Cottingham, S., Stansfield, C., Van Herwegen, J., & Anders, J. (2021). What Are the Characteristics of Effective Teacher Professional Development? A Systematic Review and Meta-Analysis. *Education Endowment Foundation*. Available at: https://educationendowmentfoundation.org.uk/education-evidence/evidence-reviews/teacher-professional-development-characteristics.

Sweller, J., Van Merrienboer, J.J.G. & Paas, F. (2019). 'Cognitive architecture and instructional design: 20 years later'. *Educational Psychology Review*, 31(2), pp.261–292.

Yoon, K.S., Duncan, T., Lee, S.W.Y., Scarloss, B. & Shapley, K. L. (2007). 'Reviewing the evidence on how teacher professional development affects student achievement'. *Issues & Answers*. REL 2007-No. 033. Regional Educational Laboratory Southwest (NJ1).

Zeichner, K.M. (1983). 'Alternative paradigms of teacher education'. *Journal of Teacher Education*, 34(3), pp.3–9.

CHAPTER 2
WHOLE SCHOOL CPD: CHALLENGES AND OPPORTUNITIES
ELISABETH BOWLING

Elisabeth Bowling is a Vice Principal at Inspiration Trust, where she works on school improvement, raising achievement and subject-specific leadership. With an MA in English Education from the Institute of Education, she is passionate about ensuring high standards in literacy and reading, as well as fostering teacher development to ensure excellent academic outcomes for children. Elisabeth has served as the lead facilitator for NIoT's NPQSL and is currently a project lead for the AI in Schools Initiative. Her dedication to advancing educational practices is evident through her work and her blog, 'A Wild Surmise,' which explores teaching and learning, EdTech and literacy.

In the ideal school, teachers are engaged in a career-long journey of professional development which engages, excites and directly influences ever-improving pupil outcomes. Staff retention rates are high because teachers feel supported to improve their classroom practice each term; they feel empowered by their growing expertise and confident their experience is valued and used in turn to support less-experienced teachers. Wellbeing and workload are carefully managed, with teachers confident that any training time is focused and efficient. Staff feel that CPD is relevant to the school's priorities and tailored to individual teachers at various stages of their careers. School priorities are clearly communicated so that the whole staff body is rowing together for the benefit of children. Professional development forms a core component of the culture of the school and enthusiasm for learning and improvement permeates every tier, from pupils, to classroom teachers, to school leaders.

So how do we get there?

We know that effective school CPD is at once vital and hard to realise. As Dylan Wiliam says, it is the 'single most effective thing' we can do to improve outcomes and decrease the attainment gap (Wiliam, 2018) and, done well, it can promote teacher retention and wellbeing (Fletcher-Wood & Zuccollo, 2020).

However, researchers find that teacher development frequently plateaus after just three years (Kraft & Papay, 2014) and school professional-development programmes often fail to prevent unhelpful teacher habits from becoming entrenched (Hobbiss, Sims & Allen, 2020). It is ironic that despite teachers being well positioned to understand how effective learning works, whole-school CPD can feel rushed, disjointed, overwhelming or divorced from perceived needs.

Running a cohesive and impactful school CPD programme is undoubtedly challenging. It requires a wealth of knowledge of school context, areas of strength and expertise gaps. School leaders need to have complete clarity about the direction of travel and the rationale behind training choices. We need to unpick the tensions and create powerful, efficient opportunities that allow teachers to improve, no matter their starting point.

And if we're honest, we've probably all encountered CPD that falls far short of the ideal. I have certainly been on both sides of sub-optimal training sessions, as a participant (a mysterious session involving shaking up a bottle of Coca-Cola springs to mind) and as a facilitator, keen to have impact but missing the mark. So, in the context of lots of CPD missed opportunities, this chapter will focus on the biggest challenges to whole-school effective CPD, and some solutions to help us reach our vision of excellent teacher development.

Consideration 1: Pre-planned vs flexible aims

When planning for whole-school CPD, the magic formula is:

clear goals + understanding of context + social support

In other words, schools must decide on and articulate specific aims for their staff, based on a nuanced understanding of need. These aims then need to be honed within rigorous structures of collaboration and reflective practice.

But what aims should be chosen? At any one time, schools have many overlapping and rapidly changing areas for development; it can be difficult to pinpoint exactly which are the areas requiring the greatest improvement. Some schools decide to buy in external packages or draw from the CPD programmes offered in other schools, but this might not always be the best idea. In a 2019 study, Kennedy found that simply importing successful PD programmes from other institutions had less impact on teacher learning than personalised, school-specific programmes (Kennedy, 2019). To me, this makes sense: the highest-leverage CPD is carefully linked to the outcomes, experience and expertise of an individual school.

It is crucial to start by identifying a problem to be addressed by staff training. The problems are likely to be evidenced through data; this same data can then be used to measure the impact of the CPD programme. If a school is at the early stages of improvement, and it's hard to know where to begin, then start with the routines that underpin successful learning environments. Once the school culture is conducive to learning, other priorities can be identified. For example, school CPD aims might look like one of the following:

Problem, informed by data	CPD aim
Teacher data show that many lessons are disrupted by poor behaviour and internal truancy is high. The current behaviour policy is inconsistently applied.	To train teachers in effective use of the behaviour system, focusing on: 1. lesson expectations and routines 2. calm, consistent responses to poor behaviour.
Children with high KS2 attainment are underachieving at GCSE, as shown by the last three years' results. Book looks have revealed low expectations for the quality of work of children with high prior attainment and learning walks show some children not working after they have finished tasks quickly.	To train teachers in ambitious and challenging teaching, focusing on: 1. effective modelling of high-quality work 2. effective classroom management whereby all children are expected to work and think hard for the whole lesson.
KS2 writing scores are well below national average. Both pupils and teachers report difficulties in writing extended pieces.	To train teachers in effective approaches to writing, focusing on: 1. shared writing approaches 2. chunking of instruction.
Sixth formers report feeling underconfident with speaking in class. Learning walks show lots of silent work with pupils reluctant to contribute to class discussions.	To train teachers in building confidence in oracy, focusing on: 1. effective scaffolds for talk 2. routines for turn and talk and cold call.

Once your aims have been identified, check that they are achievable, measurable and unlikely to overwhelm staff. When you are assured that this is the case, the CPD plan then needs to be mapped out. But is it possible to set out an entire year of training in advance? What about the unforeseen issues that pop up, or the areas for development that emerge within the school year? Balancing the tension between long-term and short-term aims remains one of the biggest challenges for school leaders in charge of CPD.

On the one hand, schools need a clear road map for staff training that encompasses, at the very least, one school year. Looking ahead encourages a cohesive plan that builds expertise across time and avoids disjointed bursts of discrete training; a long-term plan is more likely to consider how foci will be embedded into lasting practice.

On the other hand, it's essential that schools remain flexible to emerging needs. For instance, it is no good to discover an issue that is impacting children's progress and have no space to address it until the following academic year. What is the point of conducting learning walks if there is no opportunity to address the issues they raise? Why bother looking at books if time isn't then given to work on areas of development surfaced in them? Just as the best teachers are highly responsive to learners' needs in the present, an effective leader needs to remain attuned to essential issues as they emerge, without being side-tracked from an overarching vision for teacher development.

Equally, schools should remember that when CPD has had impact, pupil outcomes go up, so CPD leads are likely to be using routine monitoring procedures to check the impact of their CPD programmes, such as the following.

Shorter-term measures:

- book looks
- learning walks
- assessment scores (end-of-unit tests, quizzes).

Longer-term measures:

- SATs, GCSE results, A-level results
- standardised testing (e.g. reading age data, CATs tests).

While in isolation these measures may give an incomplete picture of learning and progress, they are useful in providing a wide-angle lens of shifting needs across time. Therefore, balancing the longer-term measures with shorter-term ones works well to check for the impact of CPD before it is too late to respond. This balance can be difficult to find, but the best CPD plans contain space for both types of measure.

Example

School A is a secondary school in Nottingham. It achieves GCSE outcomes that are slightly above the national average, and the school environment is a calm place to learn. However, the school's reading-age data from the previous year show 36% of all KS3 pupils and 48% of children eligible for pupil premium (PP) funding are reading significantly below age expectations. Cam, the assistant principal for teaching and learning, has worked with Jasmine, the principal, to identify the annual CPD goal of the school: for all teachers to be proficient teachers of reading so that more children read at age-appropriate levels by the end of KS3, and the disadvantage gap reduces. This school has fortnightly twilight CPD sessions.

Autumn term CPD	Week 1	Week 3	Week 5	Week 7	Week 9	Week 11
CPD focus	Reading: the current picture (data, concerns and solutions)	Guided reading strategies: subjects	Guided reading strategies: tutor reading	*Responsive session*	Promoting reading for pleasure	Supporting SEND

Cam has mapped out the first term's sessions and has left week 7 purposefully blank. Several members of staff have contacted Cam requesting use of this blank slot – one for training on the new register system and another for an update on working with pupils with ADHD. But Cam has stayed firm on the overarching priority for the year: to improve reading ages. He knew that he would need this session to respond to any emerging challenges, give feedback to staff about progress and refocus them.

Cam was right. Learning walks in September showed a strong start with the new reading strategies, but some teachers were struggling to generate effective text-based questions. Cam therefore dedicated the session during week 7 to clearly communicating the outcomes from the learning walk and collaboratively generating effective text-based questions for centralised reading materials. The new register system was explained via email and the ADHD strategies were communicated via the SEND weekly briefing. In this way, Cam ensured that he could remain responsive to emerging needs while maintaining the clarity of the goal.

Equally, the fortnightly structure of CPD supported Cam's vision for guided, incremental improvement in the teaching of reading across the school. After deliberate practice during each session, a gap task was set for teachers to complete before the next session as follows:

Week 1 gap task	Familiarise yourself with the reading ages of the pupils in your classes and identify those who might need support with reading. Amend your seating plans accordingly.
Week 3 gap task	Pre-plan guided-reading questions for three pieces of disciplinary text. Share the guided questions at a department meeting.
Week 5 gap task	Pre-plan guided-reading questions for two chapters of the form-time reader. Be prepared to reflect on the impact of these questions during a department meeting.

The structure of the CPD allowed Cam to support his staff step-by-step, identifying any barriers to improvement and continually monitoring progress. His CPD format gave teachers the best chance of implementing the school's aims successfully.

Planning questions:

- What are your CPD aims for the year? Why have these been chosen? What problem are they seeking to address?

- How will you structure your CPD time to best support teachers in achieving the goals?

- How are your CPD aims likely to be influenced by monitoring activities, such as learning walks, data entries, book looks and class assessments?

- How do you plan to respond when colleagues ask you for some CPD time to respond to a need they have identified?

Consideration 2: Creating cohesion

Imagine you're in your second year of teaching. Last year, your school was working on implementing a new behaviour system, which is still not fully consistent. This year, you're building your expertise through external Early Career Framework sessions which are currently focusing on effective questioning. In department meetings, your phase leader is asking you to develop writing instruction and you are teaming up with the other teacher of your year group to collaborate on effective approaches. Meanwhile, a recent school review has suggested that the school needs to make sure it is adapting learning materials so that they are accessible to all children, including those with education, health and care plans (EHCPs). And last week, your line manager dropped into your lesson and asked you to work on reviewing prior knowledge to aid recall. You don't know where to begin.

This dizzying scenario is all too familiar. With so many needs and conflicting pressures, how do school leaders keep a sharp eye on what emerges from many monitoring activities, while maintaining clarity and focus?

First, less is more. While it may be tempting to try to solve multiple concerns over the course of the year, school leaders need to avoid overloading staff. Identifying the highest-leverage goals is important in ensuring they can be reached quickly and permanently.

Second, don't be swayed. School leaders benefit from maintaining focus on the priorities. Then, any issues that arise during the year can be categorised as follows:

- Important and in line with school priorities = factor into CPD time, ensuring it is explicitly linked to current CPD aims.
- Important but not in line with current school priorities = reserve for future CPD cycles if appropriate.
- Not important or in line with current school priorities = keep in mind for future monitoring.

Third, consider how school aims can be linked to departmental goals and even wider local authority or academy trust aims.

Sometimes creating this cohesion when there are multiple goals to strive towards comes down to the clarity of communication. For example, Bethan is CPD lead of School B, a primary school in East Anglia that is part of a multi-academy trust (MAT) that oversees 12 primary schools in the region. By the end of September, Bethan was grappling with three tiers of CPD goals:

Trust aims	To improve inclusion, whereby fewer children are suspended, pupil-premium gaps are reduced and more-disadvantaged children are involved in extracurricular activities.
School aims	To improve participation and active engagement across the school so that all pupils are confident in working hard and contributing to every lesson.
Phase aims	To ensure all KS2 children improve automaticity in times tables so that more children score more highly in problem-solving activities.

At first, Bethan felt that these aims were separate from one another and should therefore be tackled individually. But upon reflection, she realised how overlapping they were and that the ultimate impact of all three was for children to be knowledgeable, included and confident in sharing their knowledge. It took some pre-planned communication to join up these aims, but she found that they supported each other well. Thinking in this way allowed Bethan to focus on the more 'upstream' issues; her team could become more preventative than responsive. Bethan started her next CPD session by narrating the aims and how they intersect:

'As a school, we know we're working hard to ensure all children are working hard and participating fully in every lesson, and we're using turn-and-talk and all-hands-up techniques to promote this. This supports our wider trust aim perfectly: for every child to feel included in the full ethos of the school. So, let's consider our phase aim now. What changes do we need to make to our teaching and curriculum to ensure every child is confident with the 12 times table? How can we check their developing confidence? How might active participation and inclusion help us here?'

Bethan found that narrating the journey of CPD – and returning to this narration at the start of each session – helped situate the goals for her staff, contributing to a greater sense of cohesion.

Finally, keep an overview of what's going on across the school. Even with the most cohesive CPD plan in the world, in practice, individuals within schools are likely to be working towards multiple aims at a time. New teachers will be following the Core Content Framework (CCF) and then the Early Career Framework (ECF). A head of department or phase lead will have carved out very specific aims for their teams to work on. The senior leadership team (SLT) will have its own set of priorities. All these activities are highly valuable. Having external curricula for teachers in the form of the CCF, ECF and National Professional Qualifications (NPQs) seems likely to have a lasting impact on overall teacher effectiveness (DfE, 2022). Whole-school CPD aims need to act like an umbrella, incorporating and directing teacher improvement activities into one cohesive whole.

The advantage of standardised external CPD, the 'golden thread' of teacher expertise, is that in theory, more time can be dedicated in school to specific areas for development. Hopefully, there will be less need to train teachers in generic approaches, such as questioning techniques or breaking down instructions, leaving more time for precise and personalised aims that are unique to individual schools. If school leaders keep up to date on the courses staff are taking, they can use this as a point of strength and draw from the expertise generated.

Your aims have been set and your plan is cohesive and sequenced. Next, you need to check that each session is relevant to all who are expected to attend.

Planning questions:

- How does your CPD plan build on previous years?
- How are you sequencing sessions to build on past sessions?
- How do whole-school CPD aims join up with departmental aims, trust-wide aims and school-monitoring processes?
- How are you avoiding overloading staff?
- How can you draw from any wider CPD activities staff are involved in?

Consideration 3: Participants

While whole-school development programmes are vital for ensuring that the members of the school community are rowing together towards the big-picture aims, evidence suggests that it is subject-specific CPD that has the most impact on teacher quality (Cordingley et al., 2018). We, therefore, need to see CPD leads give time and space for subject specialists to codify exactly how whole-school aims will be enacted in their subject/phase areas. Often, it is the middle leaders who are the best positioned to drive school improvement, and the SLT needs to support them in doing so.

A few years ago, I was tasked with improving literacy across a large secondary school. It seemed a daunting task, especially given the very different ways in which subjects approach writing and the varying confidence levels of teachers with writing instruction. I turned to the EEF for guidance and found that the first recommendation is to prioritise disciplinary literacy across the curriculum (EEF, 2018). So, my first step was to run sessions with middle leaders; each specified exactly what good literacy looks like in their subject. From here, I turned the common ground into whole-school policy, and supported subject leads to drive improvement in subject-specific expectations:

Driver	Literacy expectations	Monitoring
Departmental	Subject-specific expectations, including: • tier 2 vocabulary instruction • modelling • sentence forms • scaffolds for writing.	• Department meetings • Head of department book looks and learning walks, with support from SLT line managers
Whole school	• Presentation policy, reinforced by stickers in books. • Self-check policy, enacted by every child after any extended writing (one or more paragraphs).	• SLT learning walks • SLT book looks

Even though I built in flexibility for departments, I didn't quite go far enough. I'll never forget the end of the second literacy CPD session when one maths colleague asked me how this was relevant for her. I think she was right: I should have either clarified the relevance at the start of the session or freed up this hour for certain departments to work on more specific aims.

Whole-school vs subject specific CPD

Essentially, school leaders need to ensure the effective joining up of whole-school and departmental practices and allow for flexibility for individual departments or individuals. When planning CPD sessions, you have a few options to weigh up. Some different approaches are considered below.

Approach 1: All staff at all sessions

A primary school has found that children forget lots of previously taught content, so its CPD goal is to ensure teachers have identified core content for each topic and are able to design and deliver effective recap quizzes to enable children to recall effectively. The CPD lead decides to have all staff at every session, working together to achieve this aim. This has the benefits of clarity and efficiency. Because school leaders are working with all staff at once, they can ensure their messages are clear and undiluted. They can also check progress accurately and support staff members who might need a bit more help. The staff body feel that they are a collective, and so feelings of belonging and shared purpose are fostered. However, with lots of teachers working together, the pace is a little slow at times, and some teachers feel the training is a little generic. The examples they work on are sometimes more applicable to older children or different topics.

Approach 2: Small groups

To avoid the problems of whole-staff CPD, a CPD lead decides to group teachers by their phases. After an initial introductory session, teachers work with their key stage colleagues to identify core content for each topic and design recap quizzes appropriate to their phase. This works well to create resources that can be immediately incorporated into lessons. Newer teachers learn subject knowledge from the hands-on discussions with more experienced colleagues and misconceptions about what lesson content is the highest leverage are ironed out quickly. However, three groups are making less progress than others. In one of these groups, a few members of staff misunderstood the brief, and some time was wasted. In the other two groups, discussions are unfocused and become increasingly negative. The overall impact of the training is more variable, and at the end of the year, school leaders don't report a permanent change in teaching.

Approach 3: A cascading approach

Clearly, the best solution is a balance between having all staff meeting collectively and time allocated to colleagues working closely together to collaborate. In the scenario above, the CPD lead started each session with all staff together, modelling the focus of training. She then asked them to work in groups in the school hall, with school leaders circulating, checking and supporting. Later in the year, she regrouped staff so that teachers could learn from colleagues from different areas of the school. Misconceptions and unfocused discussions were redirected tactfully, and staff felt a collective sense of purpose. They found that protecting time for whole-school aims to be applied and practised in subject areas helped teachers apply the training to lessons more quickly.

Experienced vs novice teachers

Just as relevance to subject specialists is vital, relevance to experience level also needs to be carefully considered. We know how challenging it can be to pitch a lesson for a mixed-ability group of pupils, but this is magnified when delivering CPD to a group of adult professionals of varying backgrounds, proficiency levels, years of experience, age-group expertise, interests and values. The best CPD leads are confident in ensuring buy-in from all staff, incorporating leading voices and crafting content so that it is equally appropriate for those with 25 years of experience and those straight out of training. Some schools have sought to balance these tensions with market-place-type training sessions, where multiple members of staff offer various classroom activities for staff to sample and use as appropriate. While these kinds of sessions might have some value, they can be divorced from specific school aims and pupil outcomes. Through it all, CPD leads need to retain their wide-angle view of the school's most urgent priorities.

Solution 1: Experienced staff as facilitators

Worried about more-experienced staff feeling unmotivated by CPD? Get them involved: ask for their feedback, get them to share examples of best practice from their classrooms, see if they can coach others, or ask them to deliver staff sessions guided by your objectives. This has two benefits:

- staff are more likely to embed the CPD focus if it is being reinforced by multiple voices
- you are supporting the development of your experienced teachers by asking them to share their expertise.

Solution 2: Collaborative problem solving

You've set out your CPD aim. You've given some key tasks for staff to work on. There will undoubtedly be some knots to untangle and misconceptions to deal with. Rather than shying away from these problems, or attempting to solve them all single-handedly, why not embrace them, using staff collaboration as a tool? Ask teachers to bring the difficulties they're facing to a CPD session and use small groups across the school to problem solve. Come together as a staff body at the end to check next steps.

Solution 3: Triumvirates

My very first school created an across-school triumvirate system to support teacher development. As a newly qualified teacher (NQT), I was partnered with an experienced geography teacher and the head of Year 10, and we worked on specific tasks across the year that supported the school's annual development plan. Alongside these tasks, we were asked to drop in to each other's lessons termly and give some verbal feedback. I learned a huge amount from these experienced professionals, not only from their approaches to subject teaching but also from their high expectations of behaviour and their rapport with children. They benefited from the cross-curricular comparisons and the joining up of curriculum and pastoral approaches. With clear expectations and tasks, these across-school units can provide incredibly valuable development opportunities.

Questions:

- Are your CPD aims relevant for all members of staff? If not, what will you do about it? If so, how will you communicate the relevance?
- How will you balance a whole-school approach and a subject/phase-specific approach?
- How will you ensure more experienced members of staff are stretched by whole-school CPD?
- How will you build in opportunities for collaboration?

Consideration 4: Directing teachers' time

Many schools have a certain amount of teacher time they can direct: 1265 hours per teacher per academic year. Out of the 1265 hours, school leaders carve teaching, other duties, parents' evenings, meetings and CPD. Even schools that don't sign up to these directed hours find that dedicated time for CPD is tight. It is often the case that CPD takes the time that's left when all other activities have been organised. Nevertheless, school leaders can maximise the impact of teacher training by considering the following two questions:

1. How can we ensure that all meetings include CPD?
2. How can dedicated CPD time be structured to accelerate teacher learning?

The *when* and the *how* need to be decided.

When?

When should CPD run? Here are some of the most common options:

Frequency	Time	Duration
Weekly	INSET	Full-day/half-day session
Fortnightly	Before school	Hour
Half-termly	Twilight	30 minutes
Termly	Timetabled into the school day	15 minutes

However, CPD needn't be limited to these 'official' slots. You also need to plan the frequency of messaging. Rather than restricting CPD discussions to INSET days and twilight sessions, the most impactful programmes reinforce their messages with frequent updates, reminders and celebrations. Your planning, therefore, needs to include briefings, middle-leadership meetings, bulletins, directed-time activities, teacher feedback – every channel a school has for communication. When teacher learning is reinforced at every opportunity, teacher development becomes cultural.

How?

Teacher learning is just learning (Fletcher-Wood, 2017), and teachers are perfectly positioned to know what this should look like when done well. We know that careful practice enables training foci to be embedded into classroom delivery and work to improve pupil outcomes. Ensuring all CPD sessions are built upon deliberate practice, including actionable feedback, is the quickest way to leverage rapid progress towards goals (Berliner, 2001). You'll read more about practice in the next chapter.

In a paper by Hobbiss, Sims & Allen (2020), the researchers find that what causes many teachers to slow in their improvement across their careers is the formation of habitual behaviours that are automatic and, as such, insensitive to outcome. These habits prevent teachers from reflecting on the impact of their actions in the classroom. The teacher becomes unable to see that certain habitual behaviours are not helping a particular class, student or topic, and because of this, they are unable to change or adapt what they do in a way that might benefit pupils. A gradual increase in habitual behaviours may contribute to the fact that teachers often plateau in their development after just a few years of classroom instruction. We therefore need to encourage teachers to stay highly sensitive to cause and effect in classrooms, and we need to enable them to reflect on the outcomes of what they do. We need to prevent unhelpful, habitual teacher behaviours from forming and seek to unravel them if they do. According to Hobbiss et al., incorporating deliberate practice into CPD helps teachers 'overwrite and upgrade' existing habits.

Deliberate practice for teachers can take a variety of forms. Bambrick-Santoyo advocates the 'see it, name it, do it' approach, that involves watching an example (usually a filmed example), breaking down what was seen and then practising it, before incorporating it into a lesson (Bambrick-Santoyo, 2018). The EEF foreground four 'mechanisms' of effective professional development in their recommendations, advising CPD leads to design sessions with a balance between building staff knowledge, motivating participants, developing teaching techniques and embedding practice (EEF, 2021). Underpinning success in all these mechanisms is clear and actionable feedback.

Direct feedback about our teaching from other professionals is often missing from classrooms, especially after our first few years in the profession. Peps McCrea describes the feedback teachers do have access to as 'fuzzy': it is tricky to measure as learning is invisible, often delayed through time and it can be very hard to distinguish cause from effect in a busy classroom environment with many factors at play (McCrea, 2023). Allen and Sims argue that it is the 'problem of missing feedback from instructional choices' that helps explain why teacher development slows down after three or four years in the classroom (Allen & Sims, 2018). Effective CPD should, therefore, incorporate as many opportunities for professional feedback as possible. This might include:

- peer feedback on a script during a CPD session before a redrafted version is created
- peer feedback on a rehearsal of an interaction and a repeat
- low-stakes verbal feedback about a specific aim or goal after a learning walk by a line manager
- low-stakes emailed feedback about a specific aim or goal after a peer-observation session.

Expectations of teacher behaviour

Finally, if teacher learning is just learning, it's worth being explicit about your expectations of staff. I've seen too many CPD sessions fail because staff are on phones or laptops, they chat through explanations or they don't participate fully in tasks. These behaviours are natural: we all get distracted by tech and attempt to multitask to cross a few things off the interminable to-do list. But equally, these behaviours can be a barrier to effective teacher development. Most of the time, it's just a case of positively clarifying what you want to see from staff:

- You might want staff to sit in a seating plan, perhaps to group them by subject, experience or phase. A well-thought-out seating plan is likely to foster positive collaboration.
- You need to emphasise that sessions are to be tech free. Teachers are among the busiest people on the planet, so it is not surprising that we might want to catch up on emails or update tomorrow's lesson while we're participating in CPD. Clarifying 'no tech' at the start of the session gives staff the signal needed to engage fully in their own professional development and is likely to set up a more fruitful session.
- Be explicit about how deliberate practice should be conducted. The best sessions I've participated in model what success might look like and use tools like timers or discussion prompts to support a productive and time-efficient session.

Questions:

- How will you structure your sessions across the year? How will your chosen structure reinforce teacher learning?
- What other messaging channels can you use to reiterate key messages?
- What forms of deliberate practice will each session include?
- How will you ensure that teachers reach your expectations for learning and participation during CPD sessions?

Consideration 5: Making it permanent

If teacher learning is just learning, it requires a lasting change in long-term memory (DfE, 2019). An effective course of professional development is therefore carefully sequenced, built upon prior learning, allows for spaced reflection and deliberate practice, avoids cognitive overload, and grants time for learners to think deeply and often about the content.

Gap tasks can support the process of practice to permanence. Setting specific tasks after each session gives teachers the responsibility of trialling new approaches quickly. It's likely to keep the CPD aim at the top of the priority list.

When professional development is fully successful, content becomes part of the school life; it becomes the culture. To support this process, school leaders need to create ample opportunities to recognise, celebrate and praise (Andrews,

2011). You can embed shout-outs about excellent practice witnessed in lessons into whole-school emails, staff briefings and meetings. The more specific the praise is, and the more closely linked to CPD aims, the more likely other members of staff are to replicate the best practice showcased.

To finish, let's return to our first example: School A in Nottingham, where Cam is working with teachers to support reading instruction. Cam understood that teacher learning meant a change in his teachers' long-term memory; that he needed to build in opportunities for deliberate practice and reflection so that his teachers remained highly sensitive to the effects of their actions. His clear gap tasks allow staff to quickly embed the approaches they practice during sessions, and each of his sessions starts with participants recalling what they have previously covered. Cam remains sharply focused on the goal and uses updated reading-age data across the year to check progress and support individual children and staff where necessary. Above all, he uses all channels available to him to praise individuals and recognise successes. These include private feedback to individuals and public shout-outs in whole-school emails, bulletins and staff briefings. He makes sure staff are thinking about reading instruction at every opportunity.

The result? KS3 pupils improved their reading ages by an average of 13 months over a 10-month period. Pupil-premium children improved by an average of 17 months:

September	July
36% of all KS3 pupils are reading below age-expected levels.	20% of all KS3 pupils are reading below age-expected levels.
48% of children eligible for PP are reading below age-expected levels.	28% of children eligible for PP are reading below age-expected levels.

With clear aims, deliberate practice and careful monitoring of impact, great CPD can transform a school.

Planning questions:

- How will you ensure staff training results in a lasting change to long-term memory?
- How can you space the learning, with retrieval and gap tasks, to support teachers embedding their knowledge?
- How can you support teachers in remaining sensitive to the impact of their classroom actions?
- How will you recognise and celebrate success?

Designing effective whole-school CPD is challenging but it is powerful. It can dramatically improve pupil outcomes and inspire staff. Done well, it defines the culture of a school and ensures that every process and procedure – no matter how routine – is channelled into teacher development. As school leaders, we are privileged in our ability to recognise strong teaching and create opportunities for collaboration and professional feedback. When all teachers feel they are valued contributors to an aspirational CPD programme which is clear, efficient and provides time for practice, teacher wellbeing is supported, and pupils are the ultimate beneficiaries.

References

Allen, R. & Sims, S. (2018). *The Teacher Gap*. Abingdon: Routledge.

Andrews, H.A. (2011). 'Supporting quality teaching with recognition'. *Australian Journal of Teacher Education*, 36(12).

Bambrick-Santoyo, P. (2018). *Leverage Leadership 2.0*. San Francisco: Jossey-Bass.

Berliner, D.C. (2001). 'Learning about and learning from expert teachers'. *International Journal of Educational Research*, 35(5), pp.463–482.

Cordingley, P., Greany T., Crisp, B., Seleznyov, S., Bradbury, M. & Perry, T. (2018). 'Developing great subject teaching: Rapid evidence review of subject-specific continuing professional development in the UK'. Wellcome Trust. Available at: https://wellcome.org/sites/default/files/developing-great-subject-teaching.pdf.

DfE. (2019). 'Education inspection framework 2019: inspecting the substance of education'. Available at: https://www.gov.uk/government/consultations/education-inspection-framework-2019-inspecting-the-substance-of-education.

DfE. (2022). 'Delivering world-class teacher development'. Available at: https://www.gov.uk/government/publications/reforms-to-teacher-development.

EEF. (2018). 'Improving literacy in secondary schools'. Education Endowment Foundation. Available at: https://educationendowmentfoundation.org.uk/education-evidence/guidance-reports/literacy-ks3-ks4.

EEF. (2021). 'Effective professional development: guidance report'. Education Endowment Foundation. Available at: https://educationendowmentfoundation.org.uk/education-evidence/guidance-reports/effective-professional-development.

Fletcher-Wood, H. (2017) 'Teacher learning: it's just learning'. Available at: https://improvingteaching.co.uk/2017/10/08/teacher-learning-its-just-learning/.

Fletcher-Wood, H. & Zuccollo, J. (2020). 'The effects of high-quality professional development on teachers and students: A rapid review and meta-analysis'. Education Policy Institute and Wellcome Trust.

Hobbiss, M., Sims, S. & Allen, R. (2020). 'Habit formation limits growth in teacher effectiveness: A review of converging evidence from neuroscience and social science'. *Review of Education*, British Educational Research Association, 9(1), pp.3–23.

Kennedy, M. (2019). 'How we learn about teacher learning'. *Review of Research in Education*, 43(1), pp.138–162.

Kraft, M.A. & Papay, J.P. (2014). 'Can professional environments in schools promote teacher development? Explaining heterogeneity in returns to teaching experience'. *Educational Evaluation and Policy Analysis*, 36(4), pp.476–500. doi:10.3102/0162373713519496.

McCrae, P. (2023). 'A fuzzy feedback loop: why teaching is so hard to master'. Available at: https://snacks.pepsmccrea.com/p/fuzzy-feedback-loop.

Wiliam, D. (2018). *Creating the schools our children need: Why what we're doing now won't help much (and what we can do instead)*. York, PA, USA: Learning Sciences International.

CHAPTER 3
THE ROLE OF PRACTICE IN PROFESSIONAL DEVELOPMENT
NIMISH LAD AND LUKE BOWERS

Nimish Lad is Head of Curriculum Development for a large multi-academy trust, working on developing teachers' understanding of curriculum, assessment and pedagogy. Having previously been a Vice Principal for Curriculum and Assessment in a large secondary school, Nimish has a history of helping teachers better understand why they are teaching, what they are teaching, and how they can ensure that knowledge has been learned. Nimish is the author of *Shimamura's MARGE model of Learning In Action* (2021) and can be found on X (formerly Twitter) @nlad84.

Practice is the price you pay today to be better tomorrow.

(Clear, 2022)

Practice has long formed a core part of the professional development of many professions outside education, such as in the fields of medicine and theatre. When training to become a doctor, students are often asked to rehearse procedures, techniques and consultations. This is followed by swift and precise feedback from a more experienced colleague or coach, or someone who has greater expertise within that field (Ericsson & Pool, 2016). The same is true in the field of theatre, when actors rehearse with feedback from directors and peers prior to performance.

If we as teachers want to learn, we must engage in processes that make up effective learning. The EEF's report on effective professional development spells out the key building blocks, or mechanisms, for developing teachers (EEF, 2021). These are broken down into four main areas:

- build knowledge
- motivate teachers
- develop teacher techniques
- embed practice.

A balanced approach to professional development will include elements from all these areas. However, practice, specifically contextualised practice, can be seen as a core part of professional learning for implementing practical strategies.

In this chapter we will explore the following:

- Why do we need to practise?
- How do we develop a culture of practice?
- What myths exist around practice?
- What are the different types of practice?

Why do we need to practise?

An amateur can be satisfied with knowing a fact; a professional must know the reason why. An amateur practises until he can do a thing right, a professional until he can't do it wrong.

(Buck, 1944)

Teaching can be considered a profession where teachers are 'performing' in the classroom: explaining a concept to a large group of listeners is not unlike being spotlighted on stage to convey a message, and the method of delivery is important alongside the message, again much like a performance. In addition to the 'performance', however, teaching consists of a series of complex decisions that are played out. These decisions are a reaction to (and lead to) a range of different scenarios. Not every scenario and reaction is predictable, so teachers need to be able to respond to different outcomes. In this way, teaching is more akin to surgery than acting. Experienced teachers often develop an understanding of how pupils are likely to respond to any input, and how well they may take on board instruction or new information.

Through the process of practice as part of effective professional development, staff can build towards automaticity in their response to specific scenarios. For this to occur, we need to:

- create a bank of clearly defined scenarios
- build strategies to use in these scenarios
- engage in a process of practice and rehearsal to become automatic in using these strategies effectively.

Teachers need to be supported to be able to respond to as many scenarios as possible. By grouping scenarios into broad categories, we can develop a series of strategies, with clearly defined goals for each. The table below might help teachers and leaders aiming to develop staff to break down teaching into clear, observable scenarios that teachers within a setting can identify with. It might also be helpful if these are specific 'problems' or 'areas of improvement' that have been identified within the school. Next to each scenario, the goal spells out what the ideal end point, or 'solution', could be.

Some examples of scenarios and goals are given in the following table.

Scenario	Goal
Pupils are entering the classroom.	Control the entry of pupils into the classroom and ensure they are on task in a timely and efficient manner.
Pupils are leaving the classroom.	Control the exit of pupils from the classroom, to ensure they leave in a calm, orderly and timely manner.
Check class understanding through the use of short-answer or multiple-choice questions.	Obtain independent answers from all pupils that can be checked at a glance.
Teachers get the attention of all pupils while they are working on a task.	Gain the attention of the whole class in as short a period of time as possible.
Pupils have drifted off-task and have lost focus.	Gain the attention of the whole class, and refocus them, in as short a period of time as possible.

Each of these scenarios is a common occurrence that could happen in almost any lesson. On top of this, teaching is made up of a range of complex decisions that need to be made in the moment. These decisions need cognitive space to allow us to react optimally. This space can be created by automating some decision making. We can break down one of the broad scenarios listed above to help us better understand the need for cognitive space:

Scenario: The understanding of the class is being checked through the use of short-answer or multiple-choice questions.

Goal: Obtain independent answers from all pupils that can be checked at a glance.

Specific scenario and goal: Three multiple-choice questions will be asked, each of which has been designed to check pupils' understanding. If pupils answer correctly, they should be able to access an upcoming task independently.

There is a range of decisions that the teacher needs to make during this process. Some of these could include:

- How will I check the understanding of all pupils?

- How will I ensure that all the responses are independent?
- How will I ensure that every pupil answers?
- How can I do this in the most timely and efficient manner?
- Which pupils have answered which questions incorrectly?
- What is the root cause of their misconception/s?
- How will I correct the knowledge of pupils where misconceptions have occurred?
- How will I ensure that the misconceptions have been corrected?

The list above is only a limited range of potential questions that could occur in this scenario. To reduce teachers' cognitive load in the moment, we can consider which questions could be answered before the scenario arises (predictive questions) and which require in-the-moment thought (reactive questions). Through the process of practice, teachers' actions allow them to answer the predictive questions automatically, enabling them to focus on how they will act and react to what they find out from the reactive questions.

Predictive questions	Reactive questions
• How will I check the understanding of all pupils? • How will I ensure that all the responses are independent? • How will I ensure that every pupil answers? • How can I do this in the most timely and efficient manner? • How will I correct the knowledge of pupils where misconceptions have occurred? • How will I ensure that the misconceptions have been corrected?	• Which pupils have answered which questions incorrectly? • What is the root cause of their misconception/s?

If predictive questions can have a pre-planned response, they can be broken down into smaller actions:

- Questions are displayed on the board, one at a time.
- Pupils are given an opportunity to read the question.
- The question is read out to the pupils.
- Pupils write their answer on their mini whiteboard, ensuring that no one else can see their answer.

- Teacher calls for pupils to hover their mini whiteboard, to check they are ready.
- Teacher calls '1, 2, 3, show me' with all pupils displaying their boards at once.
- Teacher scans responses and praises positive responses.
- Reasons for the incorrect answer are obtained, with questions asked to identify the root cause of the misconception/s.
- Knowledge gaps or misconceptions which cause incorrect answer are identified and corrected. This could involve the reason for the correct answer being shared, and then repeated by the pupil(s) who got the answer wrong initially.
- Pupils who got questions incorrect are the first pupils checked during any upcoming independent, extended tasks on this area of knowledge.

Key to this thought process is the principle of going granular. In *Get Better Faster* (2016), Paul Bambrick-Santoyo uses this principle to come up with the criteria for creating the 'Right Action Step':

1. Is it observable and practice-able?
2. Is it the highest-leverage action you could ask the teacher to perform?
3. Is it bite-sized enough that the teacher could accomplish it in one week?

The list above represents sizeable actions that need to take place in a short space of time. It also does not include the incredibly complex and cognitively demanding reactive nature of unpicking incorrect answers and misconceptions that pupils may have. It makes sense to routinise as many of these actions as possible, to ensure their consistent and impactful application. This is the first reason why practice is important: it ensures that there is enough cognitive space to allow decision making – around how knowledge is building or needs to be rebuilt – to be focused on in the moment. It allows teachers' decision making to focus on the content, or 'what' is being taught, through consistent application of a process, or 'how' it is being taught and checked.

Therefore, it is important for teachers to have a repertoire of strategies to use in predictable scenarios that have been secured through the process of deliberate practice. The quality of our default reaction to each scenario, or what can be considered a habit, is crucial (Clear, 2022).

Even though a teacher may believe they have a clear and consistent way of checking the understanding of a class, it is difficult for any teacher to adjust their practice to improve it, or to gain consistency with a school-wide approach where appropriate. This leads to the second reason why practice is important: habits are easier to form than to break, and overwriting old habits is incredibly hard to do. Practice can lead to the formation of new habits.

Within the EEF's 'Effective professional development' guidance report (2021), two mechanisms refer specifically to ideas related to practice:

- Mechanism 10: Rehearsing the technique
- Mechanism 14: Prompting context-specific repetition.

Rehearsing a technique outside a classroom context allows teachers to slow a process down. They can therefore break down a technique into its component steps and ensure it is applied with fidelity (EEF, 2021). This is beneficial to department-wide and school-wide procedures, as it ensures consistency and predictability are in place for pupils.

Context-specific repetition occurs after a teacher has practised a strategy in an out-of-classroom context. They then plan to use this specific strategy within a 'live' lesson, aligned to the practised scenario. Through contextualising the practice, the likelihood of teachers seeing the benefit of the strategy, and therefore motivating themselves to continue to engage with practice, increases.

Further evidence on the importance of practice as part of the development of teaching strategies has been highlighted in the 2023 working paper from the Harvard Graduate School of Education, 'Practice-based teacher education pedagogies improve responsiveness: Evidence from a lab experiment' (Mancenido et al., 2023). The paper concludes that 'teachers can be more effectively prepared for complex teaching practices by learning in and from appropriately scaffolded opportunities to practice'. The conclusions of this paper, while carried out as part of a lab experiment, highlight the importance of modelling and rehearsal, or practice, when developing effective teaching strategies.

To summarise, practice helps to alleviate the two main issues highlighted above:

- **Cognitive space is needed for decision making**; practice can free up cognitive space by developing habits and routines.
- **Changing habits is hard to do**; practice expedites habit formation.

How do we develop a culture of practice?

Great practice is not merely a triumph of design or engineering, but a triumph of culture.

(Lemov et al., 2012)

While staff need an understanding of why they need to practice, the conditions for practice must also be in place. Lemov, Woolway and Yezzi discuss this idea in their 2012 book *Practice Perfect: 42 Rules for Getting Better at Getting Better*. They call these conditions a 'culture of practice', that can be broken down into six main ideas:

- normalise error
- break down the barriers
- make it fun
- everybody does it
- leverage peer-to-peer accountability
- praise the work.

To engage in practice, staff need to feel safe to do so. They need to be encouraged to take risks, identify errors and respond to them. When practising a specific strategy, surfacing errors is important: by explicitly practising error spotting and responding, we can normalise it, ensuring teachers feel more comfortable to practise and act on the feedback they receive.

Teachers may also find the idea of engaging in practice difficult, citing specific barriers to engaging with the process. These could include time, expertise or space. When creating a culture of practice, it is important to name any barriers and provide solutions rooted in the importance of practice.

Several solutions have been proposed to the 'time' barrier for engaging in practice. Some schools have cleared time in the timetable to allow practice to take place, while others have disaggregated time from training days over the year to allow practice to take place in 'little but often' training sessions. Thahmina Begum, executive headteacher and part of Forest Gate Community School Trust, has often spoken of a model of breaking down the time from training days (approximately 6 hours from each day) into 30-minute practice-based training sessions. By disaggregating three training days, 36 30-minute sessions are gained that can be spread throughout the year. The benefit of this model is that it ensures that there is less time between inputs of feedback, and that the feedback is in more focused 'chunks'. Begum talks about this approach, and many others, in her blog (Begum, 2023).

Barriers related to expertise can be overcome through effective modelling and the use of granular success criteria. This could be a live model or a video model. By providing clarity about what excellence looks like, expertise can be developed by allowing staff to compare their practice, or the practice they are supporting a colleague with, to the model.

Where there isn't a large enough space for all staff to engage in practice together, staff can be split into available, multiple spaces. However, if this is to be effective, experts in the processes involved must be at hand in these areas to observe and support.

Practice needs to be fun: by building in opportunities for friendly competition and incorporating elements of surprise, practice can lose the daunting feel it sometimes has, and instead become a joyful, developmental process. 'Practice should not be a punishment. When you invest the time and creativity to make practice fun, people will be motivated to participate, not only out of sheer enjoyment but also because you are communicating an important message: this is something positive that is worth our time.' (Lemov, Woolway & Yezzi, 2012).

By ensuring that everyone engages in practice, including school leaders, the importance of practice is modelled to all staff. If leaders demonstrate a model as part of the practice process, it is also an opportunity to model and practise the process of asking for, and receiving, feedback. Throughout this process, language can be used to encourage all staff to practise: 'When we all do this … When we all feed back to our partner …'.

By encouraging staff to work together and make commitments to each other, peer-to-peer accountability can be leveraged (EEF, 2021). If groups of staff can identify a granular area they need to improve on, based on feedback, teachers can hold each other to account in a supportive manner. To enable this, clear models of excellence need to be agreed across the staff body.

Praising engagement with practice, not the quality of the practice, is a good place to start when creating a culture of practice. The precision of praise is also important, and separating acknowledgment from praise can also help to build a culture of practice. Precise praise ensures that those receiving feedback are aware of exactly where they have succeeded, or they know which behaviours, or actions, to replicate. A clear process will also help to make teachers feel that their efforts with practice are being recognised.

What myths exist around practice?

The 10,000-hour rule was invented by Malcolm Gladwell who stated that "Researchers have settled on what they believe is the magic number for true expertise: 10,000 hours." Gladwell cited our research on expert musicians as a stimulus for his provocative generalisation to a magical number.

(Ericsson, 2012)

There are many myths that exist around the idea of practice. As referenced in the quote above, Malcom Gladwell in his book *Outliers* refers to the '10,000 hours rule', stating that the key to achieving expertise in any skill is a matter of practising for at least 10,000 hours (Gladwell, 2008). This statement highlights some of the misconceptions and myths that exist around the idea of deliberate practice.

Quality of practice vs quantity of practice

The quality of the practice can be considered more important than the quantity of the practice. If practice is focused on small steps that need to be improved, it is more likely to yield improvement when compared with a more general approach to practice (Ericsson & Pool, 2016).

Complexity

Some skills may take less time to master than others, and significantly less than 10,000 hours. Others may take longer. This is down to the complexity of the skill. When decomposing a skill or strategy, it is important to consider the complexity of the overall skill, and each composite step that has been created (Ericsson & Pool, 2016).

To overcome these myths, we must engage in the right types of practice.

What are the different types of practice?

Practice does not make perfect. Only perfect practice makes perfect.

(Attributed to Vince Lombardi)

Practice takes many different forms and can have different levels of effectiveness. One of the most seminal works on practice, the development of expertise and performance is Ericsson and Pool, *Peak: Secrets from the New Science of Expertise* (Ericsson & Pool, 2016).

The authors discuss three main types of practice:

- traditional practice
- purposeful practice
- deliberate practice.

Traditional practice can be considered as having an idea of what you would like to improve, so repeating it time and time again in an attempt to embed the strategy. For example: you want to improve your questioning in class, so you practice asking a variety of questions, first in an out-of-context setting and then in the context of the classroom.

Purposeful practice is where you aim to improve your ability at a specific technique by working on things that are beyond your current ability. This can be frustrating, and is often not enjoyable, but it can drive improvement. The main difference between traditional and purposeful practice is that there is a clear, granular focus, the ability to give feedback on this, and the setting of a goal. An example of purposeful practice might be that you wish to improve your questioning, so you focus on the technique of cold call. To improve your ability to cold call, you identify that you need to say the name of the student after asking the question: 'What is Newton's Third Law, Charlie?'. In the absence of an omnipresent coach, you might ask your students to check that you have been saying the name at the end of the question, rather than at the start.[3]

The most impactful and effective type of practice, as defined by Ericsson and Pool, is deliberate practice. This takes purposeful practice a step further by adding a coach or a mentor who has experience or expertise in the area of focus. If there is a clearly defined view of excellence between the mentor and the mentee, or shared by coach and coachee, then deliberate practice can be used to guide and direct practice towards this shared view. It allows the identification of the potential highest-leverage next steps towards high-level performance.

For example, you wish to improve your questioning, so you focus on the technique of cold call and discuss this with a colleague beforehand. You break down the steps required for an effective cold call and practise this out of context. The colleague observes your practice initially within the CPD session and gives live feedback which can be actioned instantly. This is then followed up in context-specific repetition.

	Traditional practice	Purposeful practice	Deliberate practice
Repetition or rehearsal	✔	✔	✔
Pushing beyond your current ability		✔	✔

---

3   If students have been trained to understand why a particular technique is implemented in a specific way, such as cold calling with the name of the student stated after the question, they can provide feedback about whether the technique was administered as intended, and if it had the desired impact. One of the goals of teaching is to promote learning in our pupils, so it can make sense to ask them to contribute to the effectiveness of the process.

	Traditional practice	Purposeful practice	Deliberate practice
Granular focus		✔	✔
Feedback		✔	✔
Setting goals		✔	✔
Agreed view of excellence			✔
Expert feedback and coaching			✔

An important point to note here is the difference between practice as part of a CPD session and live coaching, which takes place in the moment, during a lesson. Both are examples of practice and can drive development. Live coaching has the added benefit of being instantaneous and therefore minimises the damage of any poor practice, and the chance of bad habits forming. Live coaching allows for an agreed view of excellence to be modelled or prompted by the coach for the coachee in the moment. However, expert feedback is more difficult to deliver in this scenario, especially if the teacher is in the process of teaching a class of 30 pupils.

It is also important to note that as both purposeful and deliberate practice involve being pushed out of the range of your current ability, or comfort zone, they require a level of motivation, ideally intrinsic, to ensure effectiveness.

Effective deliberate practice can therefore be broken down into a cycle of:

- finding your motivation
- agreeing a model of excellence for a strategy, from which goals can be set
- rehearsing this strategy out of context in a CPD session
- receiving feedback from a coach or mentor to help decide on the next goals.

When trying to work through this cycle, it is important to consider the approach that is being taken. To help with this, the following table considers a list of questions that can be used to evaluate whether effective deliberate practice is taking place:

Motivation	How are you developing a need to succeed through the difficult process of practice?
Setting precise goals	Have the expert skills been identified? Has the overarching skill been broken down into small practice-able parts? Have goals been set that are specific, measurable, achievable, relevant and time-bound? Are these goals a challenge, and just outside your current comfort zone?
Rehearsal	Has a dedicated period of time been set aside for practice to take place? Have social conditions been created so everyone can practise in a safe place?
Feedback	Have feedback mechanisms been created to allow deliberate practice to take place? Is everything in place to allow the feedback to be granular enough to allow the person practising to stay focused on individual elements of their practice?

These questions lead to a clear process for deliberate practice to take place.

A clear process for deliberate practice (author's own).
*Feedback and re-practice should take place repeatedly until fluency; after this point a new goal can be set.
**Re-practice involves using the feedback that has been given to you by a coach and applying it to reshape and enhance the technique being applied.

As part of the feedback process, the scenario can be changed to add additional layers of complexity.

The role of practice in leadership development

While it is clear that practice can be used to rehearse 'out of your seat' situations, such as a teaching strategy, it can also be used for other scenarios that follow a clear process, such as leadership development.

Earlier in the chapter, we noted other professions that utilise practice as a high-leverage development tool. Outside of developing pedagogy, there is little evidence of this approach being considered in schools, yet the benefits of practice to developing core leadership skills, as well as other domain-specific roles, have the potential to be highly impactful.

Some examples of core practical leadership skills in which we can achieve automaticity through deliberate practice might be chairing a meeting, conducting a pupil voice panel or having a challenging conversation with a colleague.

There are over 24,000 schools in England, each open for 190 school days a year: over 4.5 million school days across the country. How many meetings are being chaired each day by leaders who have not had the chance to practise this? Without practice within this area, there is a huge amount of potential time being wasted by ineffective chairing or issues not being resolved in a timely manner. This could also damage the confidence of both leaders and staff.

Training for the many challenging conversations that are being had in schools, where it exists at all, often relies on leaders watching a training video or reading a policy. If core elements of such conversations were automated through deliberate practice, this might reduce anxiety for leaders. This might occur through a scripted range of scenarios and responses. Practice could be paused at key points to allow feedback to take place through probing questions.

Domain specific leadership practice

Imagine a scenario where, having been a successful subject leader, you've been given your first senior leadership role in leading safeguarding, attendance or behaviour. You might research the domain and plan to deliver a content-rich 'talk from the front' CPD session to staff. Alternatively, leaders might lean on the use of deliberate practice in ensuring a move towards automaticity, focusing on opportunities such as those listed in the table below:

Domain specific leadership area	Deliberate practice opportunities
Attendance	Parent phone calls Tutor conversations School attendance panels
Behaviour	Pupil transitions Behaviour routines Disciplinary panels
Safeguarding	Disclosure scenarios Conducting pupil voice interviews Active listening techniques

As a general principle in schools, what matters to the leaders, including the headteacher, is what will a) get done and b) stick. So why not use deliberate practice in all these areas?

As mentioned earlier in the chapter, the demands on a school's CPD calendar are usually significant. It must also be said that without the right culture, underpinned by psychological safety and kindness, practice can feel uncomfortable, awkward and anxiety-inducing. There is also the assumption in schools that if you are a leader you 'just know' how to do this stuff. It takes courageous leadership for a headteacher to facilitate deliberate practice with leaders on chairing a meeting or calling parents.

There are over 40,000 senior leaders currently working in schools in England and the school workforce census indicates that over 1000 a year are new to leadership. If deliberate practice became part of leadership induction processes (both core leadership and domain-specific), then we could have leaders who are able to automate processes that are currently both time consuming and challenging (DfE, 2022).

Practising leadership is almost absent in the current professional development offer in schools. Each year we recruit leaders who are well versed in utilising deliberate practice to improve performance in the classroom. Perhaps it's time we consider the same strategy to make sure that our leadership practices are just as effective as our classroom ones.

Is practice the pinnacle of improvement strategies?

Practice is proven to have an impact. Practising granular elements of a strategy, and receiving expert feedback, can lead to rapid improvements. For this reason, it is so important that we get practice right.

Practice cannot be a robotic, joyless process that is worked through time and time again. For practice to be effective, there needs to be an understanding of why it is so important; a deep understanding of whatever skill is being practised, conducted in an organisation with the right culture and conditions around practice alongside clear processes and systems. While practice may be the pinnacle of improvement strategies, it can only be as effective as the fidelity to which practice process is followed.

References

Bambrick-Santoyo, P. (2016). *Get Better Faster: A 90-day Plan for Coaching New Teachers*. San Francisco: Jossey-Bass.

Begum, T. (2024). 'Tbegumblogs'. TB blogs. Available at: https://tbeeblogs. wordpress.com/.

Buck, P.C. (1974). *Psychology for Musicians*. (12th impression.). Oxford: Oxford University Press.

Clear, J. (2022). 'The habits guide: How to build good habits and break bad ones'. Available at: https://jamesclear.com/habits.

DfE. (2022). 'School leadership in England 2010 to 2020: Characteristics and trends'. Gov.UK. Available at: https://www.gov.uk/government/publications/school-leadership-in-england-2010-to-2020-characteristics-and-trends.

EEF. (2021). 'Effective professional development: guidance report'. Education Endowment Foundation. Available at: https://educationendowmentfoundation.org.uk/education-evidence/guidance-reports/effective-professional-development.

Ericsson, A. (2002). 'Attaining excellence through deliberate practice: Insights from the study of expert performance'. In C. Desforges and R. Fox (eds), *Teaching and Learning: The Essential Readings* (pp.4–37). Blackwell Publishers. https://doi.org/10.1002/9780470690048.ch1.

Ericsson, A. (2012). 'The danger of delegating education to journalists'. Available at: https://radicalscholarship.com/2014/11/03/guest-post-the-danger-of-delegating-education-to-journalists-k-anders-ericsson/.

Ericsson, A. & Pool, R. (2016). *Peak: Secrets from the New Science of Expertise*. Boston: Houghton Mifflin Harcourt.

Gladwell, M. (2008). *Outliers: The Story of Success*. London: Little, Brown and Company.

Lemov, D., Woolway, E. & Yezzi, K. (2012). *Practice Perfect: 42 Rules for Getting Better at Getting Better*. San Francisco: Jossey-Bass.

Mancenido, Z., Hill, H.C., Coppersmith, J.G., Carter, H., Pollard, C. & Monschauer, C. (2023). 'Practice-based teacher education pedagogies improve responsiveness: Evidence from a lab experiment'. (EdWorkingPaper: 23–873). Annenberg Institute at Brown University. Available at: https://doi.org/10.26300/mm5s-b648.

CHAPTER 4

INDUCTING NEW COLLEAGUES INTO THE COMPLEXITY OF TEACHING AND LEARNING

REUBEN MOORE, ROBERT A. NASH, GEORGINA HUDSON AND LYDIA LYMPERIS

Reuben Moore MBE is Executive Director of Programmes at the National Institute of Teaching. He was previously the executive director of programme development for Teach First and a senior leader in schools and university. He was a member of the government advisory groups that created the Core Content Framework, the Early Career Framework and the National Professional Qualifications. He has had a lifelong interest in supporting teachers and leaders to develop in service of their pupils.

Dr Robert Nash is Head of Psychological Research at the National Institute of Teaching. Since completing his PhD in Psychology, he has worked as an academic in UK universities – currently as a reader in psychology at Aston University – and in these roles he has taught thousands of psychologists at undergraduate, masters and doctoral level. Rob's main areas of research expertise are human memory and educational psychology, and he has a particular interest in effective feedback processes in education.

Dr Georgina Hudson is an independent educational researcher and consultant working with school leaders and teachers across England, helping them to better understand the role of evidence in school improvement. Having completed a PhD in Education and Training, she has developed an interest in the policy trajectory of evidence-informed leadership, and has completed numerous publications and research projects in this area. Prior to her current position, Georgina supervised educators embarking on masters courses in Educational Leadership and Management.

Dr Lydia Lymperis is a research fellow at the National Institute of Teaching, and an affiliated lecturer at the University of Cambridge Faculty of Education. She has a strong interest in pedagogical innovation, teacher professional development and the role of digital technology in both. With a PhD in Education, she has been involved in various research projects in educational policy and practice, including evaluating programmes for the Department for Education and the Education Endowment Foundation, and working with UNICEF Europe and Central Asia on enhancing quality inclusive education.

Perched precariously on a sheer cliff face, Dunluce Castle in Northern Ireland has been battered by the waves for over 500 years. Having witnessed an errant ship from the Spanish Armada in the sixteenth century, and countless busloads of tourists since the start of the last century, the castle today continues to defy the natural elements: testament to its expert construction and strong foundations. When we think about building an Initial Teacher Education (ITE) curriculum for trainee teachers, Dunluce Castle does not seem an unfitting analogy. Had those blocks of stone – no matter the quality of their material or the precision of their cut – been dumped haphazardly around Northern Ireland's clifftops, the castle would certainly no longer be with us. Yet instead, the expert builders' knowledge of how best to arrange and bind the stones has ensured that the castle will outlast all of us.

In this chapter we reflect on some of the building blocks of a successful programme for those entering the profession as trainee teachers, and on how an expert builder might construct the strongest foundations and structures with those blocks that will serve teachers throughout their professional lives. While we cannot meaningfully address the countless design decisions made by ITE providers, this chapter focuses on some broad considerations of how teachers become expert in their craft, and particularly the interplay between practice and research in building this expertise. We then reflect on how 'Intensive Training and Practice' (ITAP) – a new feature of ITE programmes in England – was designed to serve these goals.

The challenges of building expertise in teaching

In reflecting on how trainees master the art and science of excellent teaching, it is important to begin by recognising that the 'basics' are by no means basic. Indeed, these foundations can be among the trickiest, most time-consuming sets of practices for new teachers to learn and establish; for many trainees, it can feel dispiriting to experience difficulty in attempting such foundational tasks. For instance, trainee teachers spend considerable time producing lesson plans which, when done well, can be invaluable. Yet every lesson plan reflects an articulation of the countless practical and pedagogical questions and challenges that any teacher faces. Planning a lesson effectively depends on trainee teachers' novice abilities to select a highly effective way to teach particular ideas to the particular pupils they serve. It might require the seeking of feedback from other colleagues who themselves have limited time for offering detailed explanations and rationales. It can also involve scouring the internet and other resources for examples and research on evidence-based practices, all of which must be evaluated critically for quality, with the potential for decision fatigue when faced with the numerous valid solutions to any given teaching problem. In summary, the apparent simplicity of lesson planning – this 'basic' foundation stone that underpins many of the advanced elements of teaching practice – belies the high level of judiciousness required.

Where does this judiciousness come from? Researchers have identified expertise as a key factor in teacher effectiveness, noting that becoming expert in making nuanced pedagogic judgements is not a linear process in practice; novice teachers can, therefore, expect this developmental process to take many years and to continue throughout their teaching career (Podolsky et al., 2019). Yet relatively few studies have explored the factors that shape teachers' ability to develop expertise while training (Lucas & Unwin, 2009). We will say more shortly about the role of establishing an evidence-informed expertise through engaging with research. But before doing so, we should not overlook the importance of direct experience, which comes in at least two complementary forms: observing and practising. With regard to the former, learning from observing more-experienced colleagues is key when building expertise (Jackson & Bruegmann, 2009), and many of us will remember fondly our earliest school mentors whose influence as role models stays with us over the years. Direct observation enables trainees to see first-hand what challenges arise in the classroom, to critically examine and deconstruct the means through which these challenges can be approached, and to reflect on how they might approach similar issues in their own future practice. Observations can also provide opportunities to engage in constructive feedback dialogue with other expert practitioners, who can help to ensure that early-career teachers develop robust teaching knowledge and skills, as well as effective working habits.

In this respect, much relies on the professional environments and support systems available to teachers, which is why mentors and mentoring-based programmes are so important for our teachers' success, even after they have completed their ITE training (Cordingley & Buckler, 2012; Podolsky et al., 2019). In England, for example, recent reforms have placed emphasis on the 'golden thread' of professional development that continues throughout a teacher's career trajectory, ensuring that mentoring and direct observation of expertise play a crucial role not only within ITE itself, but also beyond qualification. This golden thread includes the Early Career Framework (ECF), through which new teachers receive expert mentoring and developmental training throughout their first two years of practice post-qualification. It also includes various National Professional Qualifications (NPQs) that support more-experienced teachers and school leaders to refine their specialist expertise and leadership skills (DfE, 2022).

Beyond observing expert practice, there is enormous value in trainees deliberately and repeatedly practising everyday routines over time and receiving quality feedback on their practice. This practice is best supplemented by them reflecting critically on what worked, what did not work and why. Through these cycles of deliberate practice and reflection, the necessary judgements that underpin routines gradually become so familiar that trainees can make them with confidence, yet with minimal conscious effort. We think of this process as akin to chunking, as studied by cognitive scientists since the 1950s in the context of working memory and latterly drawn upon by cognitive load theorists (Miller, 1956; Sweller, 1994). Borrowing from this line of work, we know that people can handle only a finite quantity of new information at one time, but that this capacity can be expanded considerably if that same information is consolidated into meaningful 'chunks' of information: think about the difference in difficulty between memorising 12 entirely random words and memorising a coherent 12-word sentence. Other theorists think of this same process in terms of the development of schemas or scripts; these are essentially frameworks for organising procedural information based on one's prior knowledge (Schank & Abelson, 1977). When you make breakfast in the morning, for instance, it's unlikely that you ever experience the huge cognitive effort of recalling every individual step you must follow: open the cupboard, take out a bowl, place it on the countertop, and so on. Instead, you are removed of this cognitive burden because you have a well-established 'breakfast script' that you can adapt flexibly on any given morning dependent on your appetite and context.

Many key aspects of learning to teach rest on trainees 'chunking' – developing and internalising robust scripts for – everyday routines in this way. Think about the old-fashioned, yet perennially important, ritual of having pupils glue worksheets into their workbooks. Gluing stuff in requires little expert reasoning and judgement, and so as a novice ITE student, I (Reuben) never worried about the trivialities the first time I wrote at the bottom of my lesson plan 'Remind pupils to stick worksheet into the book'. Yet once I had experience of these trivialities meeting reality, I worried every single other time. Giving out the glue sticks, ensuring that the glue is applied to the correct side of the paper, ensuring the correct worksheet is stuck in the right place; all of these straightforward tasks consume precious classroom time that we, as teachers, want to spend bringing learning to life, building our young people's confidence in their understanding and application of knowledge, and discussing and consolidating their learning. Receiving simple training on how to complete these kinds of everyday rituals and routines efficiently would have equated to more of my time spent on developing the pupils' knowledge and judgement, and less time spent on giving out glue sticks. This is why it is so important that we prioritise teachers' formative ITE training for the apparent basics through observing, deconstructing and practising classroom routines that, once internalised, will expand trainees' bandwidth to focus on their more ambitious priorities.

To build their expertise, trainee teachers require access not only to practical learning environments and opportunities, but also to an evidence base. Since 2010, it has become a key priority of teacher training and professional development in the UK to build teacher expertise upon a solid foundation of empirical evidence (DfE, 2010). As part of this evidence agenda, ITE programmes' curricula have evolved over the last decade to bring into sharper focus the importance of trainees engaging with relevant research literature to inform their everyday judgements and decisions.

That said, research will rarely, if ever, provide a teacher with a unique, definitive solution to any challenge they face; instead, it will typically offer numerous possible pathways and solutions that might be considered, each with varying amounts of supporting evidence that may or may not be compelling. As a consequence, many providers of successful ITE programmes recognise that to engage successfully with research evidence, trainees require not only access to strong research evidence, but also strong research skills. Those programmes therefore include content designed to equip trainees for sourcing research evidence, making hypotheses about their classroom, thinking critically about research findings and applying them just as critically to their practice, before finally reflecting on their success and adapting their evidence-informed practice accordingly (Flores, 2018). All of this can be extraordinarily valuable, yet there is also a real danger of overwhelming ITE trainees with this research skill development, especially those whose training occurs within a postgraduate programme lasting only 10 months. The Core Content Framework (DfE, 2019) was designed with this challenge in mind. Across five core areas – behaviour management, pedagogy, curriculum, assessment and professional behaviours – the framework identifies outcomes for which trainees should 'learn that ...' (such as *'learn that learning involves a lasting change in pupils' capabilities or understanding*') and those they should 'learn how to ...' (such as '*learn how to develop fluency, by [...] observing how expert colleagues use retrieval and spaced practice to build automatic recall of key knowledge and deconstructing this approach*'). Each of these outcomes is mapped against examples of high-quality educational research to structure novices' critical reflection and practice without them being overwhelmed by extensive academic literature. As trainees' expertise grows, and as they develop more nuanced appreciations of the relationship between theory and practice, their ability to appraise the available solutions for their given context becomes more refined and more automatic (Ellis & Smith, 2017).

We have thus far considered only how to lay the largest foundation stones upon which the castle's remaining structures sit. To consider those bigger structures, let us briefly turn our attention to subject knowledge. Trainees will typically need to develop specialist knowledge in the unique building blocks of the subject or subjects they are teaching, and in how those blocks work together and relate to the foundational blocks that underpin them. Many teachers are attracted to teaching because of a love of their subject, and can be switched off when they find that some (or many) pupils do not share this same love. Yet fostering a love for a subject, helping pupils overcome the challenges of the subject and to see its beauty and its benefit, is itself a key challenge of what training to teach is about. Achieving these goals means more than having strong schemas for the foundational skills and routines we have discussed above. It also means having rich expert schemas of the subject domain, such as which complex challenges or misconceptions arise most frequently for pupils, and how they are successfully resolved.

Just as with the foundations, trainees need to approach this specialist understanding and application in a way that is grounded in evidence-based approaches. The challenge can be particularly daunting for those trainees who specialise in primary education, who are expected to cover not just one but over a dozen subjects in detail. In her book *Curriculum: Theory, Culture and the Subject Specialisms*, Ruth Ashbee (2021) lays out the building blocks of the core subjects across the curriculum, and it is fascinating to track the similarities and the differences between subjects. It provides a useful guide for teachers on how they can encapsulate their subject and therefore plan where the stones should be placed for their pupils. Still, this is easier to articulate than to do, and the level of emphasis that should be placed upon subject knowledge during ITE is hotly debated (see, for example, Daly, 2021 and Thompson, 2014). Nevertheless, pupils are entitled to learn a range of subjects, and it is highly unlikely that the foundations alone will ever suffice.

The role of research in building expertise

We have argued that engaging with research is fundamental for developing teachers' expertise, but that a challenge lies in knowing when and how much research to incorporate. As trainee teachers embark on their journeys, we often see their perceptions of research evidence vary widely: where some find it captivating, others feel overwhelmed, particularly at the onset of their training. The latter sentiment is often fuelled by their experience of research being difficult to access, offering conflicting information rather than definitive answers, and solutions that are not always immediately applicable to practice. Researchers themselves often disagree vehemently about what good 'evidence' in education should actually look like (see Perry & Morris, 2023, for an excellent synopsis and consideration of differing perspectives). For all these reasons and more, introducing trainees to research demands a strategic, iterative approach, with different methods used at different stages of their expertise growth.

Studies have explored how teachers learn to navigate this journey, suggesting that novices benefit from a highly structured and scaffolded introduction to educational research, allowing them to integrate evidence-based practice into their teaching gradually (e.g. Arends & Kilcher, 2010). Such a structured approach might begin by introducing novice teachers to the research evidence on a specific topic and supporting them to develop foundational knowledge – not only of this theory in and of itself, but also to experience applying it to their practice – before more-complex research concepts are introduced.

For instance, after learning about effective questioning techniques that are backed by research evidence, the novice teacher could be tasked with trying out those same strategies in their placement classroom, and with reflecting and seeking feedback on their efforts from their mentor. As educators progress in gaining confidence with making sound, evidence-informed judgements, gradually they should become equipped to engage with the evidence base on this same topic in closer and more critical ways. This could be, for example, by asking how those questioning techniques are adapted most effectively when working with specific social or demographic groups of pupils, or for subject-specific activities. As the trainees' sight begins to move confidently from more foundational research questions to these more nuanced research questions, opportunities arise for their research training to become more nuanced without the same risk of cognitive overload. This training might, for instance, begin to incorporate sessions on understanding research methodologies and guided practice in reading and appraising educational studies critically. Yet even at these more advanced stages, the scaffolded introduction must continue to be embedded in repeated cycles of observation, deliberate practice and feedback, allowing the novice teacher to implement their research insights directly into their classroom practice rather than experiencing them set apart from reality.

All this is easier said than done. Whereas introducing research in manageable chunks within cycles of reflective practice can help to mitigate feelings of overwhelm, simply 'mastering' individual evidence-based strategies in isolation will not in itself lead to excellent teaching. The real difficulty lies in trainees understanding the interplay between strategies and – as emphasised above – building their capacity to make sound, confident judgements about applying those strategies in combination. As the teacher training journey unfolds, ITE providers need to weave connections between the various elements of evidence-informed practice to maximise their effective application and impact.

And although certain connections, such as the link between effective explanation and formative assessment, are relatively straightforward to make, others are more complex and require thoughtful consideration. Consider, for example, the common scenario of introducing a class of pupils to a new and challenging concept. The interplay here means not merely selecting and applying a teaching technique that research shows to be effective, but also applying this technique adaptively, weaved together with other evidence-based techniques, in ways that account for the diversity in children's starting points for approaching this new concept: their abilities to retrieve their prior knowledge, to focus in class, to cope with uncertainty and getting the answer wrong, and so forth. No stone in a castle's wall is highly effective irrespective of the stones that surround it and, likewise, no evidence-based teaching technique is highly effective irrespective of the other evidence-based techniques alongside which it is embedded. Whether we are training apprentices to build monuments that last centuries, or to inspire the great minds of the future, our challenge is in supporting them to go beyond merely choosing the most effective building blocks, and to be adept at fitting these together in the most effective ways.

Intensive Training and Practice (ITAP): Cementing the principles together

To recap: a hallmark of expert teachers is their ability to act judiciously by making intuitive and informed decisions and appraising their likely effectiveness. Building this sound, expert judgement requires trainees to spend time on the basic foundations and on internalising everyday routines, to engage with research evidence, observe and deconstruct expert teaching, and use deliberate practice to experiment with and receive feedback on specific techniques. Yet when watching an expert teacher teach a class, there are simply too many things being modelled for any novice to take in. How on earth can any trainee teacher achieve these lofty goals when every lesson requires so many judicious decisions, simultaneously and in competition with other considerations and commitments? This question is precisely what a new policy introduced for ITE programmes in England – termed Intensive Training and Practice (ITAP) – seeks to address. The development of ITAP, therefore, stands as a case study of how the arguments we have articulated might be drawn together productively, and it merits elaborating in some detail.

As newly published government guidance puts it: *'The main aim of ITAP is to strengthen the link between evidence and classroom practice'* (DfE, 2023). Because teaching is a composite activity of so many different elements, there needs to be time to isolate foundational elements for focus, not least because of the inefficiencies and cognitive consequences of task-switching that are well established by scientific studies (including Grange & Houghton, 2014, and Muhmenthaler & Meier, 2019). At its core, ITAP aims to counter this problem by affording trainees opportunities to dedicate periods of their training to one foundational element at a time, with multiple blocks of ITAP each targeting a different element and totalling at least 4 weeks of a postgraduate ITE programme (or 6 weeks of an undergraduate ITE programme). In thinking about the 'intensive' characteristic of Intensive Training and Practice, many would argue that *every* week on an ITE programme is intensive. That may be true. The difference, in the authors' view, is one of quality rather than quantity: in ITAP, the intensiveness comes from this laser focus upon one single building block of the castle wall – devoting time to understanding, experiencing and working directly with this one single block repeatedly over a discrete week (or however long the ITAP block lasts) – rather than, as is common in the remaining parts of ITE, from having such a breadth of issues that must be borne in mind and juggled simultaneously.

For example, an ITAP block might – as is already the case for several ITE providers – be dedicated to scaffolding, with training focusing exclusively during that block on practices that support students as they encounter new ideas or skills. In such a block, trainees learn about the research on scaffolding, familiarise themselves with it, and then reflect on the theory behind this research. With these principles firmly in mind, they go on to observe practical examples of scaffolding being modelled, either through live or video-recorded classroom visits, and then collaboratively discuss and deconstruct what happened in those classrooms and how it relates to the research. They have opportunities to plan lessons that embed the techniques they have learned and observed, and engage in low-stakes practice of those techniques with other trainees, offering and receiving feedback as they go. And they then, of course, have opportunities to try out these approaches 'for real' in a live classroom context. Though individual ITE providers are at liberty to choose which areas of practice to focus on for ITAP in their curricula, their choices are, nevertheless, important: in our view, their choice needs to be something foundational to practice and with an established evidence base – such as questioning, scaffolding or routines – that, once secured, can form the foundational structure upon which other, more advanced, elements of teaching are built.

For Reuben, as one member of the advisory group that proposed ITAP, the ambition was to help trainees to experience a rapid sense of success with a critical aspect of teaching. Teaching is a wonderful profession and all novice teachers want to excel in it for the benefit of their pupils, yet they frequently experience a large discrepancy between the excellent teaching they observe and their difficulties in achieving the same success with their own pupils. As we have noted above, this discrepancy can be dispiriting and, at worst, can drive them out of the profession. Achieving some quick success with a single but foundational element may provide the motivation to continue. It is clearly essential to achieve this goal not through having trainees mindlessly follow instructions, or be 'blown in the wind' by popular yet ill-informed practices with weak evidence, but through supporting them to make links to underpinning evidence as they go along.

It is also important to distinguish ITAP from massed practice or 'cramming' which, as cognitive scientists have amply demonstrated, is a far inferior approach to learning than is spaced practice (for example, Kornell & Bjork, 2008). The aim of ITAP is not to treat the learning of a foundational skill as a one-shot experience, crammed and perfected within a week or so before the trainee moves on to other things. Rather, the aim is to allow space to focus on that foundational skill and to anchor it to evidence, building a robust schema that the trainee can consolidate and refine each time they return to it throughout their training and teaching journey. We feel optimistic that ITAP will prove to be a valuable tool in delivering ITE that provides trainees with the skills and strong materials they need for the remainder of their successful careers.

Conclusion

Typically, those entering the teaching profession are unaware at first of the extent of expert judgement they will need to refine. Being slow and making mistakes can be bearable, even if uncomfortable, when one takes up a new hobby or sport, yet can be devastating when embarking on what one hopes will be a long and successful career. We need to rely on more than merely a trainee's reserve of resilience to get them through their challenging training period.

The thoughtful, evidence based design of an ITE programme – embedding the right tools, techniques, deliberate practice and engagement with research in a sequence that recognises the progression from novice to expert – can go a long way to this end, and we hope to see ITAP play a transformative role. Here we have argued the priority of trainees building, from an early stage, strong and evidence-informed schemas of the everyday routines and practices that will underpin much else they do, thus freeing up the necessary time and cognitive capacity for creating effective classrooms in which children flourish. Likewise, it is not only the trainees themselves but also their ITE providers who need to be evidence-informed and, indeed, many providers continue to engage with and conduct research, to understand the best mix and sequence of steps including when, and how often, to return to them. Helping trainees to see more quickly and more frequently that their efforts deliver results might, in turn, succeed in retaining them in the profession for many years to come.

References

Arends, D. & Kilcher, A. (2010). *Teaching for Student Learning: Becoming an Accomplished Teacher*. Milton Park: Routledge.

Ashbee, R. (2021). *Curriculum: Theory, Culture and the Subject Specialisms*. Milton Park: Routledge.

Cordingley, P. & Buckler, N. (2012). 'Mentoring and coaching for teachers' continuing professional development', in S.J. Fletcher and C.A. Mullen (eds) *The SAGE Handbook of Mentoring and Coaching in Education*. Thousand Oaks, CA: Sage, pp.215–227.

Daly, C. (2021). 'Expertise in being a generalist is not what student teachers need'. IOE blog, 15 December. Available at: https://blogs.ucl.ac.uk/ioe/2021/12/15/expertise-in-being-a-generalist-is-not-what-student-teachers-need/.

DfE. (2010). 'The importance of teaching: The schools white paper 2010'. Available at: https://www.gov.uk/government/publications/the-importance-of-teaching-the-schools-white-paper-2010.

DfE. (2019). 'ITT core content framework'. Available at: https://assets.publishing.service.gov.uk/media/6061eb9cd3bf7f5cde260984/ITT_core_content_framework_.pdf.

DfE. (2022). 'Delivering world-class teacher development'. Available at: https://www.gov.uk/government/publications/reforms-to-teacher-development.

DfE (2023). 'Intensive training and practice (ITAP)'. Available at: https://www.gov.uk/government/publications/intensive-training-and-practice/intensive-training-and-practice-itap.

Ellis, S. & Smith, V. (2017). 'Assessment, teacher education and the emergence of professional expertise'. *Literacy*, 51(2), pp.84–93.

Flores, M.A. (2018). 'Linking teaching and research in initial teacher education: Knowledge mobilisation and research-informed practice'. *Journal of Education for Teaching*, 44(5), pp.621–636.

Grange, J. & Houghton, G. (eds) (2014). *Task Switching and Cognitive Control*. New York: Oxford University Press.

Jackson, C.K. & Bruegmann, E. (2009). 'Teaching students and teaching each other: The importance of peer learning for teachers'. *American Economic Journal: Applied Economics*, 1(4), pp.85–108.

Kornell, N. & Bjork, R.A. (2008). 'Learning concepts and categories: Is spacing the 'enemy of induction'?' *Psychological Science*, 19(6), pp.585–592.

Lucas, N. & Unwin, L. (2009). 'Developing teacher expertise at work: In-service trainee teachers in colleges of further education in England'. *Journal of Further and Higher Education*, 33(4), pp.423–433.

Miller, G.A. (1956). 'The magical number seven, plus or minus two: Some limits on our capacity for processing information'. *Psychological Review*, 63(2), pp.81–97.

Muhmenthaler, M.C. & Meier, B. (2019). 'Task switching hurts memory encoding'. *Experimental Psychology*, 66(1), pp.58–67.

Perry, T. & Morris, R. (2023). *A Critical Guide to Evidence-Informed Education*. London: McGraw-Hill Education (UK).

Podolsky, A., Kini, T. & Darling-Hammond, L. (2019). 'Does teaching experience increase teacher effectiveness? A review of US research'. *Journal of Professional Capital and Community*, 4(4), pp.286–308.

Schank, R.C. & Abelson, R.P. (1977). *Scripts, Plans, Goals, and Understanding: An Inquiry into Human Knowledge Structures*. Mahwah, NJ: Lawrence Erlbaum Associates.

Sweller, J. (1994). 'Cognitive load theory, learning difficulty, and instructional design'. *Learning and Instruction*, 4(4), pp.295–312.

Thompson, R. (2014). 'Initial teacher education for the education and training sector in England: development and change in generic and subject-specialist provision'. Available at https://www.gatsby.org.uk/uploads/education/reports/pdf/initial-teacher-education-for-the-education-and-training-sector.pdf.

CHAPTER 5
HOW TO PLAN YOUR SCHOOL'S CPD
SUMMER TURNER

Summer Turner is a Principal/Deputy CEO leading on education. Summer has held roles as Principal, Vice Principal and Director of Teaching and Learning within schools as well as having been a Director of Curriculum across a multi-academy trust. Summer has written extensively about curriculum, CPD and leadership, and is the author of *Bloomsbury CPD Library: Secondary Curriculum and Assessment Design*. She tweets @ragazza_inglese.

I am standing at the back of a hall watching a school lose direction. It is 4.15pm and the room is bustling; to an outsider this looks vibrant and powerful. A staff fully engaged in professional development at the end of a school day. But this great, research-informed focus that is absorbing every individual is the wrong one for the school right now. This means that not only is the school in danger of moving away from prioritising what matters but it has also wasted an hour of the staff's time, which risks losing their trust and good will. Without staff on board, there's no hope of harnessing professional development to secure better outcomes for students. It only takes one moment like this, or perhaps even the thought of a moment like this, to highlight that professional development must be driven by the strategic priorities of the school and must be planned and invested in from the very top of the school.

The opening scenario to this chapter – a staff body who will soon find out that their time has been wasted – reminds us that above all else, the profession of teaching is about people. At a fundamental level, any organisation and its leadership are driven by questions about how best to support and develop the people within it. In education, this has resonance because we are developing and supporting people in order that they might support and develop other people – both the pupils they teach and the other adults they work with. Therefore, any strategic planning must consider both the needs of the 'school' and the needs of the 'people' – in this case, the staff of a school. Knowing and being able to meet the needs of sometimes hundreds of individuals is a complex challenge. It demands an understanding of how to develop a CPD programme that is effective (i.e. it improves student outcomes), consistent but not hopelessly generic, and appealing to both groups and individuals. It requires a knowledge of domains ranging from the psychology of motivation through to the art of communication. In this chapter, I have broken down this complexity into three key problems that deserve our attention, and I will propose solutions to these problems inspired by some of the 'best bets' revealed by research.

Problem 1: Competing priorities

Solution: Refine and align school objectives with the CPD programme

This problem could also be called 'where the hell do you start?'. We are all aware of the maxim that if everything is a priority then nothing is, but we are also all guilty of being attracted by shiny things and wanting to fix everything immediately. I imagine that even reading this book has led to full pages of notes about things you want to try in your classroom or your school. At a time when the analysis surrounding teacher recruitment and retention points to 'workload, stress and burnout' as the biggest reason for teachers leaving the profession, and the reality is that professional development sits outside of 'official hours' (Hamilton et al., 2023), we need to think carefully about what sticks and what goes when it comes to CPD. This planning also requires thinking about the structural aspects of CPD, such as the use of a 'bite-sized PD model during school hours' rather than expecting CPD to take place outside of the working week (Hamilton et al., 2023).

For some teams, the de-implementation framework established in *Making Room for Impact* might be the best starting point for refining and aligning objectives both for the school as a whole and for the CPD curriculum. In this framework, Hamilton et al. propose a four-stage process for identifying and de-implementing aspects within the school, so teachers and leaders can focus more energy on work that will secure excellent outcomes for students. The de-implementation process involves removing, reducing, replacing or re-engineering aspects of school life that are costing more (whether in time, money or input) than they are contributing. The framework offers detailed steps to help schools examine how and where resources are being allocated and identify where changes can be made. When faced with a slew of demands, this offers school leaders and staff a way to prioritise the objectives that will make the biggest impact on student learning.

I deliberately combine the idea of school objectives and CPD objectives here to emphasise that a CPD programme needs to be driven by the school's needs, and equally that these objectives can only be realised by a commitment to professional development.

High quality teaching narrows the advantage gap. Crucially, it is also something that can be changed: all teachers can learn to be better

(Wiliam, 2016, Quoted in Rauch & Coe, 2019)

A starting place for producing a CPD curriculum should be the objectives of the school: 'This is what separates the content of PD of highly effective schools from the rest: they continually focus on the right things.' (Bambrick-Santoyo, 2012). Every school will have a combination of long-term goals and short-term, or reactive, goals. Ideally, schools will consequently have a long-term curriculum for CPD that contains enough flex to be able to respond to the short-term and reactive.

In their book *The CPD Curriculum,* Zoe and Mark Enser explore this concept of planning professional development through the means of a curriculum that they split into three strands: whole school, department/team development, individual development (Enser & Enser, 2021). They describe how this ideally 'should fit in with the one-year, three-year and five-year plans for the school' as well as being 'live and responsive to shifting needs'. They explore the challenges of balancing the priorities of the whole and the individual, suggesting the use of frameworks or guiding principles at a whole-school level as the starting piece of the 'jigsaw puzzle' of CPD.

Let's look at the opportunities that are presented for CPD throughout the course of the year. They might look something like the diagram below. Here we can see that there is a combination of input points and that these take place at whole-school, team and individual level. The mix of front-loaded input, regular reminders through weekly input and frequent practice creates a structure that gives space to build knowledge, motivate staff, develop teaching techniques and embed practice (EEF, 2021).

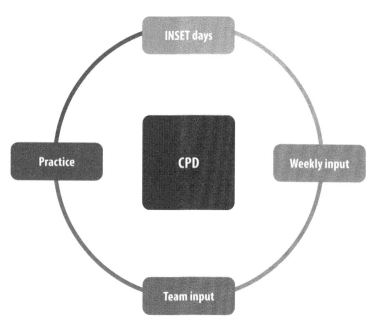

Opportunities for CPD throughout a year (author's own).

When it comes to planning the content of this CPD, it helps to gather school objectives into themes. A useful exercise to undertake can be to work with a member of the senior team (or with a whole team at the start of the year) to identify all the different competing objectives. The initial draft will produce a complex web of needs and wants, often scribbled over multiple pages. Then, slowly but surely, you begin to unpick it all, carefully exploring each tendril, noticing which are connected and which stand alone, which themes come up time and again and what simply causes a mess that can't be unpicked. Don't stop until you are left with only the essential items, the ones that beg to be on the page. Many schools will then tend to group these, often in familiar categories such as 'behaviour and attitudes' or 'personal development'. Another way you could approach it is to group them based on the common domains of a successful school such as in the diagram below.

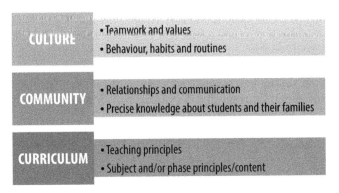

CULTURE
• Teamwork and values
• Behaviour, habits and routines

COMMUNITY
• Relationships and communication
• Precise knowledge about students and their families

CURRICULUM
• Teaching principles
• Subject and/or phase principles/content

Common domains of a successful school (author's own).

Your objectives might then fit within these categories. Long-term goals will be ambitious and complex – they might even fall dangerously close to being 'wicked problems' (Allen & White, 2019). A 'wicked problem' is a problem that is difficult to define, does not have a clear solution and is not fully solvable – so the goal itself should not be expected to be *achieved* within a short framework and is too far reaching to be a CPD priority.

An example of a long-term curriculum objective for a secondary school might be to develop a strong reading culture. This goal will have several strands that stretch over a few years and include practice in different subject areas, form time and enrichment. A rich CPD programme must, therefore, be in place to allow staff to build the relevant knowledge and practise the strategies needed to make this goal a reality (EEF, 2021). There will be short-term goals within these strands, such as making sure students are receiving extra support if they are behind their chronological reading age or setting up a form-time reading programme. If question-level analysis from a set of mock exams reveals that students are struggling to grasp vocabulary in certain questions, there might be a reactive goal around vocabulary instruction. However, what will be key is that this is grounded within the wider goal of a reading culture. While there might need to be some intense short-term work on vocabulary instruction around exam questions, the development of effective approaches to teaching vocabulary is not purely utilitarian: it is also a core component of meaningful and enjoyable reading (Sedita, 2005).

A short-term or reactive goal might need a more focused framework, such as that shown in the following figure. In the guidance report *Putting evidence to work: A school's guide to implementation*, Sharples et al. (2019) explore the implementation process, and explain how this can be used 'to help implement any school improvement decision, whether programme or practice, whole-school or targeted approach, or internal or externally generated ideas'. The guidance can be used to detail a process that might take place over a few years (if detailing a complex whole-school process) or on a much shorter timescale, if looking at a more targeted project. Professional development is sewn into the fabric of implementation throughout the process. The two cannot be separated, and the report reminds us that the most effective professional development lasts 'at least two terms, and often longer' (Sharples et al., 2019).

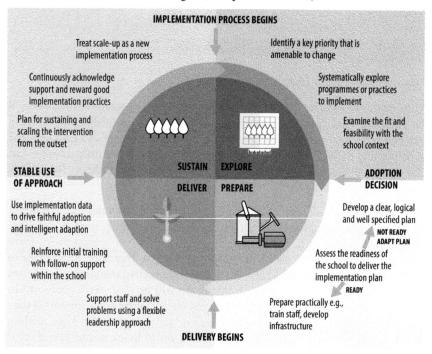

Diagram reproduced from EEF (2019) (reproduced with permission, © Education Endowment Foundation).

Another model for refining and aligning short-term objectives (and thus CPD priorities) is available in Patrick Lencioni's book *The Advantage*. Lencioni explains:

> The thematic goal is the answer to our question, what is most important, right now? [...] A thematic goal is ...
>
> Singular.
>
> Qualitative.
>
> Temporary.

Shared across the leadership team. When executives agree on their top priority, they must take collective responsibility for achieving it, even if it seems that the nature of the goal falls within one or two of the executives' regular areas of ownership.

The best way to identify a thematic goal is to answer the question, If we accomplish only one thing during the next x months, what would it be?

In this scenario, members of a senior team come together to focus on something that becomes their 'rallying cry' and has concrete short-term outcomes. A current example for many schools might be a focus on attendance; a school might set a short-term goal to improve attendance by x% over the course of a term. To achieve this shared goal, the team will need to focus on specific objectives such as: 'Increase contact with families, and speed of communication regarding attendance'. This will produce immediate CPD needs such as: training on management information system (MIS) to send text messages directly to families, or practice sessions role-playing conversations between heads of year and families. By identifying this shared thematic goal and narrowing down what needs to be achieved, you also narrow and create a sense of urgency around what should be prioritised in the 'flex part' of the CPD curriculum. This might be the part that takes place in briefings or morning meetings or can be added to team-meeting agendas for the term. Lencioni suggests that this thematic goal and its objectives can be laid out on one page alongside the everyday leadership objectives that will need to continue. This again refines thinking and allows senior teams to share this clearly and directly with staff, optimising the potential for clear messaging and a shared purpose; this makes the CPD offer more appetising for all those involved. A precise, informed and meaningful CPD curriculum can be developed through aligning the objectives with the strategic priorities of the school, but without staff buy-in, you will fall at the first hurdle. This is the motivation for tackling problems 2 and 3.

Problem 2: Genericism

Solution: Co-construct CPD thread with middle leaders and maximise time for subject/phase specific CPD

One of the challenges highlighted when refining and aligning objectives is that when these are designed by a senior team, they tend to fall into the generic. While these generic objectives can be made more specific by exploring the ways in which they manifest in different teams, this leaves us with a couple of challenges:

- How does a senior team ensure that the CPD at this level meets with the school's expectations for effective professional development?

- How does the CPD curriculum address the specific objectives of teams and individuals within the school?

We also are left with a provocation when we consider the effects of communities of practice (such as subject and phase communities) in professional development, and how these can be harnessed successfully:

> *By allowing communities of practice to not only form and collaborate but also to flourish beyond the borders of their own boundaries, educational institutions can harness a very powerful and old form of knowledge creation and also empower their own members at the same time.*

(Kirschner & Hendrick, 2020)

This leads us neatly to a potential solution which is to look at ways in which you can draw on the expertise of your middle leadership to develop a CPD curriculum thread that builds in space for communities of practice to engage and construct parts of the offer. This will also benefit individuals when we consider the learning potential of participating in social communities and the development of professional identities that is realised through this participation (Lave & Wenger, 1991).

At my school, members of the senior team think carefully about what we can learn from middle leaders to develop the most effective professional development. The avenues for this learning include line management, middle leadership meetings and surveys alongside the more informal conversations that happen within the work environment. It might follow a process like that shown in the figure below, which is a rough version of the process undertaken by my senior team. The power of this back and forth between middle leaders and senior leaders is twofold: you gain meaningful insight into the needs of the school that senior leaders might not see themselves and you bring together a rich mixture of knowledge domains (see Lock, S. ed., 2020/Barker & Rees, 2022, for more on why considering knowledge domains is key to effective school leadership).

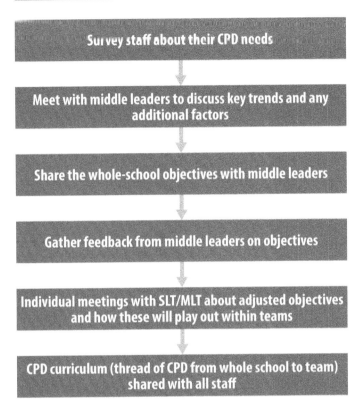

Survey staff about their CPD needs

↓

Meet with middle leaders to discuss key trends and any additional factors

↓

Share the whole-school objectives with middle leaders

↓

Gather feedback from middle leaders on objectives

↓

Individual meetings with SLT/MLT about adjusted objectives and how these will play out within teams

↓

CPD curriculum (thread of CPD from whole school to team) shared with all staff

A co-creation process (author's own).

As part of this process, we also ran sessions on what effective CPD should look like, starting with a two-part training slot and practice opportunity for the SLT before re-running this with middle leaders. This not only ensures we are all more knowledgeable and able to be consistent in our approach to CPD but that we have a shared language that can inform line-management conversations and add a layer of shared accountability.

As part of our dedication to communities of practice, we knew that the CPD thread had to include regular time for departments to meet and practise beyond the usual department admin time. We had been long-time advocates of the importance of subjects at secondary agreeing that 'discipline identities and subject subculture of high school teaching are critical contexts for defining shared work and building communities of practice' (McLaughlin & Talbert, 2001). Indeed, as someone who has worked on the development of curricula across primary and secondary schools, there is great value and learning to be had from subject communities at primary as well.

We decided to build department-time into the school day, ensuring that the timetable allowed for there to be one period a week when the team would be able to have an hour together. We looked at the case study from Fran Hayes at Durrington High School (Enser, 2021) where departments have fortnightly 'subject planning and development sessions' (Spdss). These sessions are focused on developing subject and/or pedagogical knowledge in a specific area identified through department checks on student learning. The purpose of these sessions is targeted and focused directly on improving students' performance in individual subjects and building the knowledge base for the department staff. We took this idea and considered how we could ensure this was woven into our school's CPD thread.

As a school, one of our goals was to consider how to learn more from Young's version of powerful knowledge and the idea of student engagement with that knowledge.

> *If you haven't encouraged students to engage in the process of acquiring knowledge, which is a very difficult process, then all you get is memorisation and reproduction in tests. I think this is why a lot of kids actually lose the desire to know during their time at school, whereas if we somehow found a way of enabling kids to discover that desire, which is inherent in all of them, schooling would be quite different. It would be a lovely thing to be a teacher.*

> (Young, 2022)

We knew our students were becoming very confident at learning and re-iterating core knowledge, but we wanted to further develop their relationship to that knowledge. We had several whole-school sessions about this, first introducing the ideas and theory then giving practical examples. This included selecting three areas that a department team could look at as part of their CPD thread: developing teacher subject knowledge; reviewing and tweaking their curriculum; developing pedagogical approaches to encourage student participation. These were followed up by department sessions where middle leaders guided staff to focus on a specific component such as use of turn and talks (pedagogy), reviewing the opportunities given for applying knowledge in a specific unit (curriculum) or co-planning a tricky content area (subject knowledge development).

We gathered feedback throughout this cycle of CPD and made the following tweaks in response.

- Introduced more guided practical examples from the start (we had wanted to give autonomy to departments, but found many wanted more specific examples to get them started).

- Shared models of great use of subject development sessions to help less-experienced heads of department.

- Developed a clear set of questions and expectations for line-management meetings to ensure middle and senior leaders worked well together to create professional development that linked meaningfully to whole-school priorities, was precise and gave room for practice to embed changes.

- Gave departments a steer about using alternate meetings to look at department administration (some departments noted that they needed some space for admin but didn't want to return to this absorbing all their meeting time), and emerging priorities that didn't fit within the planned CPD thread.

Like all models, and to keep with the theme of always being better, there are still areas that we want to develop further but this has been an illuminating way to add specificity to our model while also striving for common goals.

Problem 3: Improvement requires change

Solution: Attach short-term goals to long-term path, and plan with staff psychology in mind

As a school leader, you are presented with the dilemma that school improvement may require change but that change (especially in a profession that often suffers from change overload from sources both external and internal to the school) can take a toll on staff. You have a responsibility as a leader to create a culture in which both students and staff thrive; in fact, I would argue that without the latter it is hard to sustain the former. Change for change's sake is irresponsible but resisting needed change because of fear is also unacceptable. When planning CPD, this understanding of change is vital because every piece of professional development can feel like an addition. Let's imagine the psychology of a staff member when interacting with a school's CPD programme.

Soraya, a primary school teacher, has been teaching for 10 years – six of which have been at School A. In that time, there have been multiple education secretaries, there have been reformed performance measures at KS1 and KS2, a new Ofsted framework and the school has just joined a multi-academy trust with a centralised curriculum offer. Two years ago, Soraya's CPD was focused on using oracy approaches to develop writing with her Year 5 students, and she led a research project on the work she did on this within her class. But the following year, the school decided they needed to focus more on embedding grammar practice into creative writing, so Soraya had to develop new schemes of work and the deputy head led a year-long programme of CPD about how to use these effectively. When Soraya returned to school in September, she was told that she must now use the centralised curriculum resources provided and that CPD sessions are being led by the trust's English lead and are focused on using tier 2 vocabulary to improve writing. The senior team emphasised that the centralised resources would reduce workload and that as the school was still underperforming when it came to KS2 writing, it was great that staff would get professional development on writing.

It is not hard to see why Soraya might become disillusioned with the idea of professional development even if the quality of the individual sessions is high. There is nothing wrong with any of the foci mentioned in this scenario, and it is likely that the senior team felt that these were priorities at the time. However, Soraya is facing multiple changes from assessment to curriculum at both a national and local level. Before she even has the time to think about her own development needs within the school priorities, she must get her head around new content and new approaches. The senior team has clearly identified writing as an area to develop in the school so there is a consistency, but the approaches and forms of development have changed every year. There is also a sense in which this CPD is being done *to* Soraya rather than involving her – what happened to the research project or the schemes of work she has developed or the 10 years of expertise she has built up to this moment? Even if the current focus on tier 2 vocabulary is the right one to improve students' writing, it will be hard to persuade Soraya that this isn't just another initiative.

It is likely that staff will feel more motivated to embrace change if they feel some ownership of the process (Ryan & Deci, 2017). The co-construction of CPD between senior and middle leaders will help with this ownership but it is also worth considering how to involve the full spectrum of staff without losing sight of school priorities. Staff are more motivated by a school's goals when these are transparent and consistent. Therefore, the challenge is to ensure you have clearly developed long-term goals that are shared and embraced by the staff body as well as more-specific short-term goals that can be responsive to need. A senior team's job is to ensure that the long-term goals are over-communicated and that there is clarity as to how short-term goals fit into the wider picture. Imagine the difference if in the summer term, the senior team in School A had met with staff such as Soraya and asked her what she had learnt from the CPD she had experienced in the last few years, and what else she needed. If, following this, the senior team had considered explaining the journey of the school and the links between the different approaches to writing, or been honest about why they had turned away from any of their former positions, they would have started to give the staff a reason to buy-in.

It is leaders who 'create an organisational climate that is conducive to change' (Sharples, Albers & Fraser, 2019) and part of this is understanding that 'messaging is not so much an intellectual process as an emotional one' (Lencioni, 2012). Staff need to feel trusted, safe and listened to, and they need the reassurance that comes from consistent and clear messaging.

Effective messaging is easier when you a) have clarity about your goals and b) know your staff. There is general agreement that 'great professional development starts with knowledge about what teachers need' (Bambrick-Santoyo, 2012). It is a senior leader's role to gather this knowledge. This will likely come from the range of qualitative and quantitative data gathered throughout a school year, such as assessments, learning walks and book scrutinies. Bambrick-Santoyo explores how the precision of this data gathering allows for more tailored professional development: the senior leader reviews observation data and identifies checks for understanding as a focus for CPD, inviting teachers to attend if this was something they were struggling with in their classroom. 'Teachers are happier, because they know that if a leader asks them to attend a workshop, it will address something they personally need' (Bambrick-Santoyo, 2012). This can be used both to identify areas for development in teaching and in student culture. In the schools in *Leverage Leadership*, this data is gathered through 'culture walkthroughs' – a culture version of learning walks – where staff observe break times or school routines such as line ups to see how they meet the school expectations.

In this model, data is gathered primarily by senior leaders, with the precision ensuring that it does capture what staff need from CPD which helps to motivate staff. It is worth senior teams considering how to involve staff directly in the development of the programme. Mark Leswell describes a focus on this at scale from a trust central team: 'Our approach involved polling teachers on the main challenges for their students, and then developing CPD pathways that use research evidence to address these challenges' (Leswell, 2023). Teachers bring their knowledge of the school areas for improvement to the table and the role of the trust (or school) is to develop research-informed pathways that respond to this need. This sits alongside an instructional coaching programme to help 'create new habits for teachers' and a video library of research to encourage staff to build their professional knowledge.

Both approaches aim to address the idea that professional development must include a combination of input and follow up, while understanding that 'professional development processes are unlikely to be successful without also ensuring there is high-quality content and a sharp focus on pupil outcomes' (Sharples, Albers & Fraser, 2019). These aims for effective professional development should also lead to staff engagement. Staff are more likely to feel motivated and inspired by professional development if it is embedded, high-quality and they are given the chance to be successful in implementing new or adjusted strategies. The EEF also addresses the importance of communication and repetition: 'The content of professional development activities should also be aligned and purposeful so that individual learning activities collectively reinforce one another and revisit the same messages' (Sharples, Albers & Fraser, 2019).

While most of this chapter has been concerned with the over-arching plan for CPD, it is worth noting that the quality of this planning will be undermined if you do not think about the content and format of CPD in specific detail. Teachers' frustrations with CPD often come from the offer being low-quality or not being sustained. It is understandably frustrating to attend even excellent CPD if you are never given the chance to put this into practice or if you are given a couple of chances, and are then moved on to the next 'development opportunity'. We need to approach professional development as a form of learning in which we want to build long-term knowledge and develop new habits, and we know this takes time and practice.

In *Leverage Leadership*, Bambrick-Santoyo explores the way to develop objectives that allow CPD sessions to be successful. A useful example on student culture shows how narrow a focus needs to be for it to be successful:

Weak: Too Broad

- Understand the characteristics of students who struggle to follow directions.

Weak: Still Too Broad

- Identify methods to help struggling students follow directions.

Strong: Specific and Bite-Sized

- Implement one of three techniques for redirecting a student who is struggling to follow directions.

(Bambrick-Santoyo, 2012)

I know I've certainly been guilty of running CPD which fits in that 'still too broad' category and been frustrated when I've come to the end of a session and realised that I've overloaded my audience and will have to revisit this again. But the reality is you often don't have the time to revisit it, or the lack of specificity leads to frustrations as staff struggle to implement this directly into their practice.

To avoid these hiccups, Becky Allen (Allen, 2019) suggests three questions that senior leaders should ask themselves about their CPD sessions:

1. What is the objective of the session and is there any plausible route by which it could lead to improved instructional practice?
2. Are the delivery methods likely to lead to something being learnt?
3. How will new ideas get established into the repertoire?

This is planning not simply with staff emotional psychology in mind but also with cognitive psychology – applying our understanding of how people learn to make sure professional development improves the quality of teaching. Allen suggests that these questions guide us to certain formats of CPD that are more tailored, such as instructional coaching and lesson study, although she accepts that schools often do not have the resources to make these work effectively. A starting point is to create the type of CPD that teachers 'believe is useful' and the working conditions that make them 'feel like they want to get better at teaching' (Allen, 2019).

It is this final point that resonates and sits at the heart of what senior leaders need to be thinking about when it comes to CPD. Leadership creates the culture that determines whether staff will take professional development seriously. If we believe that it is this development that can improve the quality of teaching and, therefore, the outcomes for our students, we have a moral responsibility to look at professional development as so much more than the sessions that run on a Wednesday afternoon. It is creating the conditions in which people, be it staff or students, can flourish.

References

Allen, B. (2019). 'Improving teachers' instructional practice: Critically important, but incredibly hard to do'. In C. Scutt and S. Harrison (eds) *Teacher CPD: International Trends, Opportunities and Challenges*, Chartered College of Teaching.

Allen, B. (2019) 'Musings on education policy: Careering towards a curriculum crash?'. Available at: https://rebeccaallen.co.uk/2019/12/04/careering-towards-a-curriculum-crash/.

Bambrick-Santoyo, P. (2012). *Leverage Leadership: A Practical Guide to Building Exceptional Schools*. San Francisco: Jossey-Bass.

Barker, J. & Rees, T. (2020). 'Developing school leadership'. In S. Lock (ed) *The researchED Guide to Leadership: An Evidence-informed Guide for Teachers*. Woodbridge: John Catt Educational Limited.

Barker, J. & Rees, T. (2022). 'School leadership expertise: What is it and how do we develop it?'. Ambition Institute.

EEF. (2021). 'Effective professional development: guidance report'. Education Endowment Foundation. Available at: https://educationendowmentfoundation. org.uk/education-evidence/guidance-reports/effective-professional-development.

Enser, M. & Enser, Z. (2021). *The CPD Curriculum: Creating Conditions for Growth*. Carmarthen, Wales: Crown House Publishing Ltd.

Hamilton, A., Hattie, J. and Wiliam, D. (2023). *Making Room for Impact: A De-Implementation Guide for Educators*. California: Corwin Press, Inc.

Kirschner, P.A. & Hendrick, C. (2020). *How Learning Happens: Seminal Works in Educational Psychology and What They Mean in Practice*. London: Routledge.

Lave, J. & Wenger, E. (1991). *Situated Learning: Legitimate Peripheral Participation*. Cambridge: Cambridge University Press.

Lencioni, P. (2012). *The Advantage: Why Organizational Health Trumps Everything Else in Business*. San Francisco: Jossey-Bass.

Leswell, M. (2023). 'Enhancing teacher quality through research-engaged professional learning and development: A scalable approach'. *Impact: Journal of the Chartered College of Teaching*. Issue 19.

McLaughlin, M.W. & Talbert, J.E. (2001). *Professional Communities and the Work of High School Teaching*. Chicago: University of Chicago Press.

Rauch, C.J. & Coe, R. (2019). 'Evaluating and measuring teaching quality'. In C. Scutt and S. Harrison (eds) *Teacher CPD: International Trends, Opportunities and Challenges*, Chartered College of Teaching.

Ryan, R.M. & Deci, E.L. (2017). *Self-Determination Theory: Basic Psychological Needs in Motivation, Development, and Wellness*. New York: The Guilford Press.

Sedita, J. (2005). 'Effective vocabulary instruction'. *Insights on Learning Disabilities*, 2(1), pp.33–45.

Sharples, J., Albers, B. & Fraser, S. (2019). 'Putting evidence to work: A school's guide to implementation. Guidance report'. Education Endowment Fund (EEF). Available at: https://dera.ioe.ac.uk/id/eprint/31088/1/EEF-Implementation-Guidance-Report.pdf.

Young, M. (2022). 'What we've got wrong about knowledge and curriculum'. TES Magazine. Available at: https://www.tes.com/magazine/teaching-learning/general/michael-young-powerful-knowledge-curriculum.

CHAPTER 6
WHAT MAKES A SUCCESSFUL INSET DAY?
MADELEINE FRESKO-BROWN

Madeleine Fresko-Brown is a vice principal in a large London secondary academy, in charge of teaching and learning and curriculum. She has led on teacher development and CPD in various guises since 2017 across two different academies, as well as initial teacher training in a third. As part of these roles, she estimates that she has planned, curated and/or delivered sessions in approximately 18 INSET days. She can sometimes be found on X (formerly Twitter) at @M_X_F.

INSET: In-Service Education and Training. Incredibly Stressful and Exhausting Timetabling. Inevitably Sleep-Encouraging Talking …

Whatever INSET means to you, it has no guarantee of being a success – by which we should mean, improving teaching practice. While there's very little recent and relevant research on INSET days specifically, we can draw on well-known research and understanding about professional development, learning and cognition more broadly to give us some guidance.

To reduce your cognitive load, if you take only two things away from this chapter, please let them be:

1. Plan your INSET days well in advance.
2. Apply everything you already know about good teaching and teacher development to the way INSET days are planned and delivered.

This chapter aims to provide guidance for those charged with planning INSET, as well as offering useful context for heads and other members of senior and middle leadership involved in planning, delivering or attending INSET days.

Question 1: How many INSET days, and when?

In England and Scotland, most maintained schools are expected to provide five INSET days in an academic year (DfE, 2023b); in Wales, this has been increased to six until the end of 2025 (Welsh Statutory Instruments (WSI), 2023). Academies and free schools have more freedom to choose how many non-teaching days they provide, but all schools and academies face the question: how many days to run as whole INSET days, and how many to 'disaggregate', shifting six hours of training (a full INSET day) to after-school 'twilight' CPD time, and also giving staff the benefit of non-working days in lieu to account for these.

Unsurprisingly, there is no research to tell us what is the 'right' number of days. Some schools choose to run all five as whole day INSETs, others disaggregate some. However, given findings that professional development is most effective when participants are afforded 'frequent, meaningful engagement' with training (Teacher Development Trust (TDT), 2015), it is reasonable to assume that disaggregating at least some days is a gamble worth taking: enabling the school to run 12–18 hours of twilight time, two or three after-school sessions, per half term. It is worth here acknowledging union guidance that 'disaggregated INSET days will only be used with the agreement of staff and the recognised trade unions in the school, following an equality impact assessment' (NASUWT (The Teachers' Union), 2022). Twilight CPD sessions usually mean extending the working day and directed time for staff, so this should be considered carefully and consulted on, especially if it is a new approach.

Better than starting with numbers of days or numbers of hours, planning for INSET and CPD time should be done holistically, starting with needs and school priorities:

1. What are our priorities?
2. What are our staff training needs?
3. What staff training time do we need to achieve these?
4. When would this best be placed?

The NPQ Leading Teacher Development framework stresses the importance of 'providing clarity on where content fits into school improvement priorities and, where appropriate, a wider curriculum for professional development' (DfE, 2020). Keeping these priorities front and centre will help to ensure meaningful INSET planning.

While these questions are a fine place to start, anyone who has tried planning this way will know that staff development plans often have to flex to fit things we absolutely *have* to cover, whether that be mandatory training or the miscellany necessary for the smooth running of a school. We'll explore this in more depth later in this chapter.

In terms of when, almost all schools choose to place at least one, sometimes two, INSET days at the beginning of September, to induct new staff and ensure the whole staff body is 'on the same page' in terms of school routines and priorities for the year to come. Other INSET day placement varies more widely, with some going for a beginning of every term approach, and others placing them at harder-to-predict points. Aberdeen, for example, has an INSET day in August (the beginning of term), then mid-term in November, February and May.[4]

One school I worked in always had an INSET on the first Friday of July. This INSET doubled up as an induction day for new joiners, and allowed the teaching and learning team to launch the whole-school priorities for the following academic year. We found this a fruitful time in many respects: everyone was happy to have a shorter teaching week in July, new staff felt fully included in plans going forward, and it also reduced the cognitive load inherent to September INSET days by bringing the teaching and learning focus forward.

Question 2: What are the aims of INSET days?

A vital question to answer, and to seek agreement within a senior team before beginning to plan any INSET day, is 'What are we trying to achieve?'.

INSET days are so broad and ill-defined nationally, they may reasonably take on any of the below aims, and more:

1. To develop staff knowledge of a particular programme, pedagogy, subject content or other skills/knowledge relevant to their role.

2. To accelerate pupil progress, for example through analysis of recent assessments and discussion of individual results and actions arising from these.

3. To deliver important information that all staff need to know, such as safeguarding, health and safety, GDPR (General Data Protection Regulation), school policies and processes.

4. To build a school culture or ethos around a certain priority.

5. Some mix of any/all of the above.

The EEF, in its 'Effective professional development guidance report', takes the first aim as its central focus, by telling us to: 'Ensure that professional development effectively builds knowledge, motivates staff, develops teaching techniques, and embeds practice' (EEF, 2021).

---

4   A correspondent from Aberdeen council informed me that 'These are generally linked to holiday weekends, where they can, to help parents plan childcare. They are also spaced to support delivery of the school improvement plan'; see also https://www.aberdeencity.gov. uk/services/education-and-childcare/view-school-term-and-holiday-dates.

In a recent paper, Sam Sims et al. suggest two purposes to professional development: one, to provide insight, defined as 'teachers gaining a deeper understanding of how teaching and learning occur in the classroom', and two, to build teachers' motivation to change (Sims et al., 2023). Much literature around teacher professional development focuses exclusively on improving teaching quality. In an earlier paper, which was used as the basis for the EEF professional development recommendations, Sims et al. define teacher professional development as 'structured, facilitated activity for teachers intended to increase their teaching ability' (Sims et al., 2021).

Readers of this chapter who have been responsible for planning INSET days may recognise a conflict here: all the theory and best practice suggest that the focus of our professional development should be on improving the quality of teaching directly, however there are several other training needs inherent to working in a school that are not captured within this definition. The following section will begin to address these.

Question 3: What must, and what should, we cover?

There is no single, centralised list of mandatory training but The Key (2023), a national information service for school leaders, has a helpful document that summarises the essential sections of training as follows:

1. Safeguarding
2. Health and safety
3. First aid and medical conditions
4. Data protection
5. Special educational needs (SEN) and looked after children (LAC) (for designated staff).

If each of these was given an hour in each annual September INSET, that's a whole day used up straight away. INSET can be a valuable time to focus as a whole staff body on school priorities without the distractions of a school day, so spending this day solely on mandatory compliance training is likely to feel less than impactful. There is, therefore, a need to plan ahead and to be creative with how and when this mandatory training is delivered. While some of it (safeguarding) must come at the beginning of the year, other mandatory training (health and safety, data protection) can be delivered more flexibly – perhaps via video, using an online platform, or at another point in the term.

In addition to considering mandatory training, a leader coordinating CPD will need to discuss INSET priorities with senior leaders and coordinate requests for

INSET time from various colleagues. To evaluate these requests, the questions in the first section of this chapter about school priorities are most pertinent, along with the agreed aims of the INSET day. CPD leads are advised to start these conversations far in advance – ideally several months before the INSET in question – mapping out the time, and always leaving a little in reserve to enable the accommodation of any unforeseen circumstances.

Where there are various other CPD opportunities available throughout the year, an important question to discuss as a team is what do we want to 'front load'? Tom Bennett suggests that the most successful schools feature:

- clarity of culture
- detailed expectations
- staff engagement
- attention to detail
- consistent practices.

While Bennett reminds us that 'professional development does not only occur in discrete quanta such as external training days or INSETs' (Bennett, 2017), it may well be that if culture and behaviour are a priority for your school, frontloading them in a September INSET should be your driving force to ensure this clarity from day one.

Question 4: Who should speak on INSET days?

One major decision in planning an INSET day revolves around who will deliver the content. Will it be members of your senior leadership team, middle leaders or lead practitioners with specific specialisms, classroom teachers or even external speakers?

External speakers can be appealing as they may project an air of credibility to your audience. However, guest speakers are rarely mentioned in the literature as a factor of successful development, and certainly not in isolation. An external expert may provide some insight or motivation to staff, but for this to translate into action in classrooms, it will require careful follow up from the team on the ground in school.

Greg Ashman, teacher and education researcher, suggests the following questions to consider when booking an external speaker:

1. Are they presenting their own ideas or someone else's?
2. Are or were they a teacher? If so, were they a success? How do you know?

3. What, if any, evidence base is there for the ideas they are presenting?

4. Do you want the presentation to be motivational or substantive? Does the speaker match your aim?

5. Are the ideas things that can be practically implemented or are they more abstract?

6. Does the speaker match the audience e.g. have you invited PE teachers to a talk about teaching algebra?

(Ashman, 2023, reproduced with permission)

Whatever the answers to the questions above, two very important questions to consider will be whether the external speaker or provider is using the mechanisms set out in the EEF guidance (which apply to internally- and externally-designed CPD alike), and how they or you will follow up and monitor any changes in practice that are expected to come out of this presentation.

In terms of who from within school is best placed to deliver INSET sessions, credibility and ability to motivate are both important factors. School leaders should consider how to distribute the leadership of the school's priorities effectively so that middle leaders have buy-in and can provide insight and motivation to colleagues (Bektaş et al., 2020). The EEF mentions the importance of modelling in good professional development, citing an example of a school that uses 'a teacher to lead delivery, to give examples, and work with staff to deliver that training. I think we find that it is more authentic if it comes from someone who is teaching a full timetable.' (EEF, 2021)

Question 5: How should we plan and deliver INSET sessions?

While many of the above considerations may be ultimately out of your control as a CPD lead, the 'how' of the sessions is where you can really make a difference. If you have this role because of your expertise and experience in the area of teaching and learning, here is your chance to really shine and show you can practise what you preach, with adults as well as children.

Frequent are the complaints of being 'talked at' for too long on an INSET day, cognitive overload and, ultimately, boredom. But these are not inevitable. With careful planning and guidelines for delivery, your INSET days can be transformed into engaging, motivating experiences for your staff body. How? By taking what you already know about cognitive science, good teaching and how we learn, and applying it to your audience.

a) Manage cognitive load

Most educators will be familiar with at least some aspect of cognitive load theory (Sweller, 1988). Yet a common complaint of teachers is that INSET days are cognitively overwhelming. The desire to fit as much training as possible into a day can sometimes supersede sensible decisions about how much is too much. Cognitive load theory tells us that our working memory can remember and process up to four new items at a time (Cowan, 2001). This can increase if schemas in the long-term memory are activated.

According to Kalyuga et al. (2011), 'the main factor that determines the amount of cognitive load that learners experience is prior knowledge'. Teacher educators face a difficulty here because in a typical INSET scenario, we are faced with teachers with prior knowledge and experience of teaching ranging from six weeks to 36 years or more.

School leaders require more than a surface understanding of cognitive load theory to make good decisions. For example, the theory suggests that using worked examples is a good way to reduce cognitive load, especially among novice learners. However, a recent study in Tanzania by Timothy et al. (2023) with pre-service science teachers compared worked examples with a problem-solving instructional design. Researchers hypothesised that worked examples would create lesser cognitive load and lead to better performance in the task (identifying scientific misconceptions). However, the opposite was found to be true. The researchers commented that 'the findings are consistent with Chernikova et al. (2020) who found that less advanced learners might benefit more from scaffolding support with a high level of guidance (examples) than more advanced learners for whom self-regulated learning (problem-solving) is the best instructional strategy' (Timothy et al., 2023).

As well as instructional design, INSET organisers will need to consider the time span of any content delivery. A 2008 study by Maureen Murphy used a repeated-measures design to evaluate how well participants learned and retained content delivered in a one-hour session compared to three 20-minute chunks. On all measures, Murphy found statistically significant improved reactions, and higher scores in the post-test and the knowledge-retention test 30 days later, when content was taught in three 20-minute chunks with a five-minute break after each chunk (Murphy, 2008).

Clearly there are no easy answers when it comes to cognitive load in teacher development, but, based on the theory, there are a few best bets that can be applied to INSET instructional design:

1. **Careful scheduling**: have a break after every session and don't let any session run for more than one hour, unless it is particularly interactive. Include some department time or individual planning time in the schedule to allow people to process and apply what they have been learning. Coffee and snacks in break times help too. There is genuine research on the benefits of coffee breaks: Waber et al. (2010) found that the strength of an individual's social group at work improved when coffee breaks were taken at the same time as colleagues.

2. **Advice to presenters**: advise presenters to have ideally one, and a maximum of three, main takeaways for their session. You could provide guidance based on the Murphy study above that three chunks of 20 minutes are optimal for attention and learning. Check their slides in advance to see whether they have stuck to this, and ask them to rehearse timings. Where appropriate, each takeaway needs some application time or deliberate practice to make it stick (Lemov et al., 2012).

3. **EEF recommendations to reduce cognitive load**: remove less-relevant content; focus only on the most-relevant content; vary the presentation via the use of multiple examples; employ strategies such as dual coding (the combination of verbal and visual instruction) (EEF, 2021).

b) Revisit prior learning

In their 2014 book *Make it Stick*, Brown et al. elaborated on and further popularised research into pupil learning. They suggested that students remember things better when they are regularly tested on them, and that the most effective form of testing is spaced out and interleaved with other material. While arguably, teachers have got better at deliberately planning retrieval into classroom curriculum plans, the use of retrieval in staff professional development, and particularly INSET days, has lagged behind.

With INSET days being so spaced out, they can provide a good in-built opportunity for retrieval of core school priorities and the strategies in place to address them, yet anecdotal evidence suggests that schools often fall into the trap of treating each day in a stand-alone way. The EEF argues for carefully planned retrieval to be built into teacher training, with 'revisiting prior learning' listed as a core mechanism for effective professional development. The EEF cites a US study that employed a deliberate spiral curriculum in developing teachers' skills around English language development in grades four and five (Abe et al., 2012). However, a critical reader might notice that this programme entailed 42 days of professional development over two years – a quantity of CPD time we can barely imagine, let alone be able to set aside for the development of one subject skill in primary school.

Retrieval practice is just as important for adults as it is for children. If something you're saying in an INSET is worth saying in the first place, then it is surely worth remembering. Some opportunities for doing this are below:

1. **Quizzing**: everyone loves a quiz! Giving staff a quiz will help motivate them to recall material and make the information stick better for longer. Our most recent September safeguarding session was followed up by an online quiz (of things covered in the session and also in *Keeping Children Safe in Education* (DfE, 2023a)) a couple of weeks later, allowing for time to forget and then retrieve the material. The quiz also provided a diagnostic for our safeguarding lead to provide further clarification and updates via our staff bulletin.

2. **Look back and look forward**: plan opportunities to revisit important material from previous INSETs, and ensure you have an ongoing CPD model that will revisit the learning introduced on an INSET day.

3. **Build collective schemas as a staff body, and continually revisit these**: visuals, prompts or cues may be useful here; another effective mechanism mentioned in the EEF guidance (2021). Whatever concepts have been introduced in an INSET day need to become an ingrained way of working over time, to the point where it is no longer a cognitive effort to remember them.

c) Boredom

Teachers might not be as visibly disruptive as pupils, but I challenge you to find an INSET day across the country where staff aren't occasionally taking a peek at their mobile phones. But, as with cognitive overload, boredom is not inevitable.

Several of the mechanisms in the EEF guidance involve active tasks that ensure that teachers are not passive recipients of CPD but will be actively involved. These include rehearsal, action planning, self-monitoring and context-specific repetition (EEF, 2021). Some of the above points, such as regular breaks and quizzing, will help keep boredom at bay, and there are some even more active things you can do too, while avoiding gimmicks:

1. **Give teachers something to do**: many of us were taught in our teacher training that when planning a lesson we should always consider 'what is the teacher doing?' and 'what are the pupils doing?'. The same principle should apply here, yet it is far too common to see an INSET session planned with little regard to what the audience are supposed

to be doing with the information they are receiving. Aware that her session involved a lot of information delivery, our head of sixth form planned a worksheet for staff, with several questions, the answers to which could be found throughout the presentation. Motivated by a box of chocolates, the PE team were extremely diligent and engaged in the session, taking home the prize and enjoying themselves at the same time!

2. **Give them something to say**: who is delivering your INSET sessions? Is it all senior leaders? Where do teaching staff come into this? How about teaching assistants? In our school, with the guidance of the SENDCO, learning support assistants lead small-group discussions about specific pupils with SEND, with teachers chipping in to offer strategies and guidance (in line with best practice advice (Foster, 2019)). As well as having more credibility if guidance is coming from someone 'at the coal face', involving a range of colleagues helps prevent boredom – for the presenters themselves, and for everyone else invested in what they have to say. On a practical note, involving others means you need to plan much further ahead, so ensure you factor this in.

3. **Give them somewhere (else) to be**: if your INSET plan involves having all staff together in the hall for the entire day, you need to rethink it. Even with the most engaging sessions, most adults will struggle to withstand this quantity of 'all-staff' content. All INSET days should involve some break-out sessions, whether by department, key stage or year group areas (again, ensure you plan ahead and give the leads enough time to prepare), or in action research groups, coaching pairs, or teaching-and-learning communities (Gibson & Mader, 2019). The EEF mentions action planning as a key mechanism for effective development days, so these smaller-group opportunities could be an opportunity for this.

Question 6: What do support staff do during INSET?

Continuing with the theme of planning, I would encourage CPD leads to think about support staff as integral to your INSET planning, rather than as a bolt-on or an afterthought. I have already mentioned teaching assistants and learning support assistants who, as well as delivering some CPD of their own, are always invited to any CPD aimed at teaching staff in my current school. Where you have other student-facing support staff (such as behaviour mentors, student support officers or non-teaching heads of year), how are they involved in and developed by your INSET?

Have you considered the training needs of your non-student-facing support staff? In all schools, all support staff (along with site-, cleaning- and canteen teams) should be invited to safeguarding training and data-protection training. (Data breaches are often more likely to come from the staff who spend the most time processing student data.) Beyond this, such staff are likely to have training needs for their roles that can be sometimes neglected in schools. INSET days can provide opportunities to offer support staff bespoke training, for example on administration systems they may regularly use. Support staff often also say that they would benefit from more training on managing student behaviour around the school, and on what to do should an incident arise.

A teaching-and-learning CPD lead need not take on this additional workload of planning support-staff INSET alone. Reach out to senior support staff, such as the office manager or support-staff line managers, to identify the training and development needs for their team, and how they can help to address these needs given, say, half a day of INSET time. You might find that the simple act of speaking to them in advance, and explicitly including support staff in the scheduling, will make a world of difference to the way support staff feel valued and acknowledged within the school community.

Conclusion

Even if done well, INSET days are unlikely to transform your school overnight. What they can do is help set a positive staff culture of continual improvement and professional learning, get all staff on the same page with regards to particular school priorities, and start to upskill staff on a particular area of pedagogy or subject knowledge, with the continuation of this running through the academic year in CPD.

References

Abe, Y., Thomas, V., Sinicrope, C. & Gee, K.A. (2012). *Effects of the Pacific CHILD Professional Development Program. Final Report* (NCEE 2013–4002), National Center for Education Evaluation and Regional Assistance. Available at: https://ies.ed.gov/ncee/edlabs/regions/pacific/pdf/REL_20134002.pdf.

Ashman, G. (2023). on X (formerly Twitter). Available at: https://x.com/greg_ashman/status/1740448281199886431?s=20.

Bektaş, F., Kilinç, A.Ç. & Gümüş, S. (2020). 'The effects of distributed leadership on teacher professional learning: mediating roles of teacher trust in principal and teacher motivation'. *Educational Studies*, 48(185), pp.1–23.

Bennett, T. (2017). 'Creating a culture: How school leaders can optimise behaviour'. An independent review of behaviour in schools'. DfE. Available at: https://assets.publishing.service.gov.uk/media/5a7506e4ed915d3c7d529cec/ Tom_Bennett_Independent_Review_of_Behaviour_in_Schools.pdf.

Brown, P.C., Roediger III, H.L. & McDaniel, M.A. (2014). *Make it Stick: The Science of Successful Learning*. Cambridge, Massachusetts: The Belknap Press of Harvard University Press.

Chernikova, O., Heitzmann, N., Fink, M.C., Timothy, V., Seidel, T., Fischer, F. & DFG Research Group COSIMA. (2020). 'Facilitating diagnostic competences in higher education: A meta-analysis in medical and teacher education'. *Educational Psychology Review*, 32(1), pp.157–196.

Cowan, N. (2001). 'The magical number 4 in short-term memory: A reconsideration of mental storage capacity'. *Behavioral and Brain Sciences*, 24(1), pp.87–114.

DfE. (2020). 'National Professional Qualification (NPQ): Leading teacher development framework'. Available at: https://assets.publishing.service.gov. uk/government/uploads/system/uploads/attachment_data/file/925511/NPQ_ Leading_Teacher_Development.pdf.

DfE. (2023a). 'Keeping children safe in education 2023'. Available at: https:// assets.publishing.service.gov.uk/media/64f0a68ea78c5f000dc6f3b2/Keeping_ children_safe_in_education_2023.pdf.

DfE. (2023b). 'School teachers' pay and conditions document 2023 and guidance on school teachers' pay and conditions'. Available at: https://www.gov.uk/government/publications/school-teachers-pay-and-conditions.

EEF. (2021). 'Effective professional development: guidance report'. Education Endowment Foundation. Available at: https://educationendowmentfoundation. org.uk/education-evidence/guidance-reports/effective-professional-development.

Foster, H. (2019). 'Teaching assistants: The right ethos, good CPD and effective deployment'. Headteacher Update. Available at: https://www.headteacher-update.com/content/best-practice/teaching-assistants-the-right-ethos-good-cpd-and-effective-deployment.

Gibson, C. & Mader, S. (2019). 'Building teaching and learning communities: Creating shared meaning and purpose. ACRL. Available at: https://www. alastore.ala.org/content/building-teaching-and-learning-communities-creating-shared-meaning-and-purpose.

Kalyuga, S., Ayres, P., Chandler, P. & Sweller, J. (2011). 'The expertise reversal effect'. *Educational Psychologist*, 38(1), pp.23–31. doi: 10.1007/978-1-4419-8126-4_12.

Lemov, D., Woolway, E. & Yezzi, K. (2012). *Practice Perfect: 42 Rules for Getting Better at Getting Better.* San Francisco: Jossey-Bass.

Murphy, M. (2008). 'Matching workplace training to adult attention span to improve learner reaction, learning score, and retention (Microlearning)'. *Journal of Instruction Delivery Systems,* 22(2), pp.6–13.

NASUWT. (2022). 'Directed time checklist'. Available at: https://www.nasuwt. org.uk/static/f41c4e7e-89ee-4d28-b57db239d2e32949/7f8daf82-c8e8-43e1-8c7ad22397de4b66/Directed-Time-Checklist-England.pdf.

Sims, S., Fletcher-Wood, H., O'Mara-Eves, A., Cottingham, S., Stansfield, C., Van Herwegen, J. & Anders, J. (2021). 'What are the characteristics of effective teacher professional development: A systematic review and meta-analysis'. London: Education Endowment Foundation. Available at: https://educationendowmentfoundation.org.uk/educationevidence/evidence-reviews/teacher-professional-development-characteristics.

Sims, S., Fletcher-Wood, H., O'Mara-Eves, A., Cottingham, S., Stansfield, C., Goodrich, J., Van Herwegen, J. & Anders, J. (2023). 'Effective teacher professional development: New theory and a meta-analytic test'. *Review of Educational Research.* Available at: https://doi.org/10.3102/00346543231217480.

Sweller, J. (1988). 'Cognitive load during problem solving: Effects on learning'. *Cognitive Science,* 12(2), pp.257–285.

Teacher Development Trust (TDT). (2015). 'Developing great teaching'. Available at: https://tdtrust.org/about/dgt.

The Key. (2023). 'Mandatory training for school staff'. Available at: https://schoolleaders.thekeysupport.com/staff/staff-ratios-and-qualification-requirements/teaching-roles/mandatory-training-for-school-staff/?marker=full-search-q-mandatory%20training-result-1.

Timothy, V., Fischer, F., Watzka, B., Girwidz, R. & Stadler, M. (2023). 'Applying cognitive load theory in teacher education'. *Psychological Test Adaptation and Development,* 4(1). Available at: https://econtent.hogrefe.com/doi/10.1027/2698-1866/a000052#.

Waber, B., Olguin, D., Kim, T. & Pentland, A. (2010). 'Productivity through coffee breaks: Changing social networks by changing break structure'. *SSRN Electronic Journal.*

Welsh Statutory Instruments (WSI). (2023). 'The education (school day and school year) (Wales) (amendment) regulations 2023. Available at: https://www.legislation.gov.uk/wsi/2023/37?view=plain.

CHAPTER 7
WHY DOES COACHING SERVE OUR MOST VULNERABLE?
JENNY THOMPSON

Jenny Thompson is Executive Director at Dixons Academies Trust, working both directly with schools and on trust and sector-wide development. Jenny travelled and worked overseas before becoming an English teacher, SENCo and school leader; she was Principal of Dixons Trinity Academy in Bradford. During her first maternity leave, Jenny was appointed behaviour adviser for the Department for Education and completed post graduate studies in the application of AI in education. Jenny was a member of the design group for the Independent Review of Children's Social Care and is currently a member of the Government's Cultural Education Plan panel and part of CST's Trust-led School Improvement Inquiry. Jenny has also co-authored a chapter in ReseachEd's Guide to Leadership.

I approach the topic of coaching for professional growth with self-awareness: I have a two-year-old and a four-year-old and I am trying to hold down an executive role. My life is drowning not waving; although, it is possible that having been forced to recognise my own working limits and finite capacity has served to create a mandate over the past few years about needing to rely on others and getting better at supporting others. And seeing strength, and finding purpose, in that.

I used to give education all of my thinking space, all of myself, and the job, as I had formulated it, remained impossible. Now, as a parent, I can only give what I can and it turns out (who knew?) that I was not, in fact, the deciding factor. Too many leaders in our sector treat experience-won knowledge as precious and are, at times, unwilling to share it as they (consciously or otherwise) perceive it as their credibility. This is machismo. This is bravado. Coaching for professional growth shifts this paradigm into a healthier space: pushing power down. Taking the knowledge out of the heads of the few and into the heads of the many is the intersection of coaching and self-determination: it facilitates highly effective and highly ambitious autonomy, and it amplifies efficacy.

How do we help all teachers get better?

The answer to educational leadership cannot be 'hero teachers'. What a sorry disservice to the many and varied attributes of our colleagues. If we are all needed, especially at this moment where recruitment is so tough, and if we are all welcome, then we all deserve to grow and learn.

So, how do we help all teachers get better, especially when we know that getting better takes time? From where do we get this time? Our sector needs capacity and brilliance – two things that rarely coalesce – so it will take radical action to generate.

First, as leaders, we have to know what the job of teaching is in our school. What I connect to great teaching will be different from that of another leader or another team member. Sometimes fundamentally, sometimes minimally, sometimes by intent. We may argue that the increasingly astute commitment to research-informed practice mitigates this, but it is indisputably the case that to fit everything we now need into the same time we ever had, we need to be able to stop time.

A thought experiment

So, for a moment, let us pause (we will pick this back up) and delve into the thought experiment of a single teacher in a single classroom in a school. We can assume, for the purposes of this thought, that cognitive science is now so hackneyed as to be everywhere all of the time. Let us also assume that in this school, it is untainted by mutation.

Let us imagine a teaching team of 30 in this school. All teachers are taught the key theories of cognitive science; we can assume, therefore, that intelligent sequencing, retention and spaced practice have been delivered effectively. The teachers get it. They understand it. But whole-school routines have not been designed around it.

The job of the teacher, then, is not just to implement their understanding of cognitive science, but also to design the routines through which this understanding will be iterated in their classroom. And not just to design the routines but also to teach them to their children and re-teach them until they are embedded. Which will be hard because no one else in the building will be reinforcing them; indeed, other teachers might be reinforcing completely different routines and expectations.

In a secondary setting, where a child could easily have 10 different teachers in a week, that is not just asking the child to manage the learning of the content across their curriculum but also to learn and retain the expectations of the routines (and all the subtle and complex differences) in each classroom with each staff member. This cognitive burden will diminish, for the child, the capacity to learn and retain the content of the curriculum; for the teacher, the time taken to embed their lone routine is time lost from content delivery. We understand about the cognitive burden for children. But it is also true for staff: the cognitive burden; the professional burden. Again, there is only so much capacity. Great ideas and great research become squished and squandered through incoherent implementation: 'reducing within-school variation in value added between subjects would have 10 times more impact on overall attainment when compared to moving schools below the floor standard to just above it' (Treadaway, 2019).

How do we challenge in-school variation? How do we establish consistency of culture? How do we directly impact on practice in every classroom every day? How do we become ready to face any storm? We identify what works and then we coach at whole-school and individual level to deliver change that is both systemic and specific; built and bespoke. Only a school this intentional will deliver for SEND and only coaching can fathom the specificity necessary to improve teaching and learning consistently.

Let's head upstream

To know what to do to close the disadvantage gap sincerely and systematically, we first need to look at where energy and resource are typically spent without consistent impact; most often this is in the classroom – the 'classic approach' to tackling disadvantage. This approach often requires teachers to give extra attention to pupil-premium students, for example. Lots of these phrases will sound familiar and they are smattered across almost every pupil-premium strategy statement: identifying pupil-premium students on seating plans, marking their books first or asking them more questions.

Yet in our resource-limited, stretched-budget environment there is likely a better space to focus. So why don't we? Because it is upstream, and upstream (outside the school gates in the multi-agency work of civic support and social care and policy) is unfamiliar; it feels too far away from the fire-fighting of now. And also (please do not be offended) because of us: our skill-set gaps. Only in the rigour of great order can the vulnerable minority become the focus.

The cost of not making a leadership decision is likely to be greater than that of making a less-than-hyper-perfect decision. Drucker presented this as the 'effective' decision: so many school plans fall down in the shift from what is 'right' to the actions needed to achieve this (Drucker, 1967). As the leaders in this thought experiment, we need to make decisions about how we are going to maximise the use of cognitive science. We need to set up some whole-school routines.

These whole-school routines can form the basis of our instructional coaching, the practice that we do as a team: planned, sequenced, but also highly responsive. Our quality assurance (in whatever form we have decided that should take) can track the efficacy of the routines that have been constructed around cognitive science and direct the planned instructional coaching practice or feed into highly responsive edits to the plan – the 'yikes, we need to work on this, it isn't embedded!' leadership-feedback moments. It is a question of what we want our teachers to spend their time on. Their time is precious; it is finite.

Systems create capacity

Through systemisation, our teachers do not need to be the designers of routines. Instead, they can depend upon the whole-school structures that enable their precious time to be spent on subject specialism, on expertise, on appreciation and professional growth of their whole authentic self, but also on the whole-authentic selves of the children we serve. This is where we want teachers to face their professional capacity: on expert adaptive practice that scaffolds to ensure every child can make accelerated progress. Of course, the risk here is a generation of teaching-automatons: unable to think or feel; unable to see past the curriculum and into caring about our children.

This is why coaching needs to hold both hands: whole-school routine guidance that creates safety and predictability for our children, and deep personal connection between colleagues; the power of checking in. Relationships are both the foundation and the progeny of highly successful professional growth, and their relative strength shifts intent, shapes communication and alters everything.

So often when coaching arises in a discussion about school improvement, the knee-jerk response is 'but we have no experts to draw upon'. This is a common challenge: how do we develop the mechanisms of coaching alongside developing the expertise necessary to direct teachers' growth? The answer sits in the most humane and mundane: it's just sequence. Start by demystifying the expectations. If, in those early conversations, the ask is to establish relationships, then the habit of talking is formed in trust. Then, as the routines and systems of the academy are articulated, shared and refined, there is functionality to learn, look at and improve together. Build the relationships that will navigate the routines into automaticity. This is why coaching for professional growth is agnostic: it does not judge your philosophy of education, it is just a secure and sincere delivery method.

Professional growth at Dixons

So, at Dixons, what do we do? Every colleague has professional growth coaching at least, in the early stages, once a month. (In many of our schools, where coaching is embedded, it takes place weekly.) This time is sacrosanct and it is timetabled. It is not a phony 'last 10 minutes' of line management. It is a real commitment. As such, we have had to design new time into old systems. We use large-group teaching to free up teaching loads, and we do this knowing that the growth a teacher achieves in the half hour away from their children will become a benchmark for efficacy. That is a high bar and a considerable burden for our Centre for Growth's training offer. Rightly, we take it seriously.

As such, the Centre for Growth has thought deeply about coaching to ensure that we can talk about it simply. We have delivered training to every staff member in Dixons on how to be both coach and coachee. Every academy leader is held to account for ensuring this commitment is met and that bespoke support is drawn upon.

Everyone at Dixons is supported to keep getting better through regular and intensive coaching check-ins. At its most simple, coaching helps colleagues to get better at their work and usually involves colleagues focusing on embedding a weekly, actionable and specific step, or goal-setting and problem-solving, with the help of a coach.

An early mistake we made was assuming that the duration of focus on an individual step would match the frequency of the coaching – a step would be prescribed each week. We soon acknowledged this as folly – sometimes the same intractable but high-leverage step will need to remain the focus for much longer. When coaching staff more expert in a domain, the coaching approach may often move to be problem-based and practice-light, while for staff at developing stages of expertise, a more directive, practice-rich approach may be typical (EEF, 2021).

Deliberate practice forms an important active ingredient of coaching at Dixons. Colleagues, particularly those with less expertise in a domain, spend less time discussing and more time reviewing a model: rehearsing and responding to bespoke feedback. With staff who have greater expertise in a domain, reflection and learning will be facilitated using tools and techniques such as active listening, powerful questions and presence (Deans for Impact, 2016). Everyone, irrespective of expertise, has an accompanying 'zoom out' conversation each term to ensure their growth looks beyond the minutiae and we keep a shared understanding of where the coachee wants to be, to ensure we are aligned.

Who will coaching support?

It is more than a decade since the introduction of pupil-premium funding yet students from the lowest-income homes still do not progress as well as their peers: 'in 2023 the gap had widened' (Ofqual, 2023). In the 2022/23 academic year, pupil-premium students made up a quarter of the population of mainstream secondary schools. This is not tinkering-round-the-edges stuff. And, of course, students with SEND are more than twice as likely to be eligible for free school meals. Efforts to close the disadvantage gap will never outrun SEND progress. By all and any measure, national data is telling us that tirelessly well-intentioned interventions are not shifting the dial: 'Progress 8 scores for SEN and non-SEN pupils showed that non-SEN pupils averaged a Progress 8 score of 0.10 whereas SEN pupils averaged a Progress 8 score of –0.62. This means non-SEN pupils, on average, progressed more than expected when compared with similar pupils in their prior attainment group, whereas SEN pupils achieved around two thirds of a grade less than expected by the end of KS4' (Gov.UK, 2024, © Crown Copyright).

Our most vulnerable are deserving of our best. They should be where our thinking begins. But schools are full of chaos and complexity – as is any organisation full of complex humans. Coaching is a system that, when intentional and coherent, creates typicality out of turmoil: routines are embedded, language is shared and in-school variation is diminished. And in that typicality is safety: a safety that speaks first to our most vulnerable.

Let us imagine a turnaround setting. Let us imagine that a teacher in this setting may well be a highly skilled practitioner. Let us imagine that there are 30 children in the class (just one of that teacher's classes) and that eight of the children are identified as children with SEND. That teacher is teaching four lessons that day consisting of four different classes so is, perhaps, considering the needs of around 30 or so students with SEND. Let us imagine that the teaching resources are available and of quality.

Let us assume that, in this school, leader(s) have fallen foul of the fundamental misconception of individualisation. Instead of seeing the value of individualisation sitting in the personal relationship with the student, they have misinterpreted it as the need to have highly personalised adaptations documented for each child. Without being shaken and really looked at, this approach can be recounted as a brilliant step forward. In high-accountability, the narrative can be more tempting than the truth. And how many of those highly personalised adaptations might actually be deliverable? By going too specific, they no longer become navigable. They simply will not happen. And that will not be the fault of the teacher.

Instead, imagine that whole-school strategies and routines have been decided upon that draw highest-leverage adaptive strategies into the main offer. Imagine also that a small number of highly curated, practised, embedded approaches sit alongside this. These strategies and approaches could be recorded in grouped documentation. This then makes the role of that expertise that has been brought in free from desk-bound hours and up and in the community of the school. This would mean that the expertise would no longer be trapped in front of a screen on a desk: instead, the expert could be adding capacity in the community of the school.

Highly personalised documentation is, in reality, undeliverable in classrooms. With enormous capacity, it may be navigable in planning but not in the live decision-making of every classroom, every day. And there is no enormous capacity, so it is also unmaintainable. It will be a single point of time when this level of specificity is accurate. As economist John Maynard Keynes would have it, by 'overstepping the limits of the possible, [it] has in practice settled nothing' (Keynes, 1920). Instead, by focusing on a small number of high-leverage strategies and routines that can be pulled into the daily main offer, all children will be supported, leaving genuine capacity for the highest-value nuanced delivery where it is genuinely required. Quality-assure this instead: flex your practice to support any routines that need to be re-embedded or reviewed.

Importantly, to land the systems through coaching, we need sincere relationships: remember, holding both hands. A Harvard study found that frequent, regular check-ins with managers improved performance, which is no surprise (Twaronite, 2019). The study's truly amazing finding was that the conversation did not have to focus on a particular task or skill. I feel this is finally justification for all the cups of tea I have had with our team over the years! Any type of interaction – even an informal conversation about family or the weather – lifted performance. That is the power of interaction; the power of checking in. And, when we reflect on it, of course this is true. Of course, we do better when we feel we are among valued colleagues and friends and when we feel valued too.

Culture is shared practice, shared language, shared ways, hows and whys. It is the reduction of the daily experience of in-school variation. Its delivery mechanism is coaching. In the high winds of a school in turnaround, as the guy ropes fail, the tarpaulin flails and the bitter wind and rain tear through, we struggle to feel safe – let alone feeling rested, joyful or able to reflect. Think of coaching as the passing on of information about how to put the tent up well in the first place. Coaching is calm, sequenced, considered guidance from an expert. Think of practice as getting to trial all those skills on a fine day far away from the moment of the storm. And think of the supportive learning walks as the kit checks that make sure the guys and pegs are all secure before the night falls. So much is done away from the moment of crisis that, when it occurs, the tent holds out and everyone inside passes through it unharmed, often unaware of what has swirled around them. And anyone who has ever taken little ones camping knows how much more true this is for our most vulnerable!

When I originally took on school leadership, I thought that it would be full of strategy and the business of management. In fact, I was not sure I would like it. The bit I had always loved about my job was the kids and the families and the love and tears and growth together. What I should have realised, of course, is that leading a team *is* about all those classic fundamentals of organisational leadership – but it is really about the births, deaths and marriages you hold each other through. It is about sharing your lives together and appreciating one another: learning and living through one another. Coaching: checking on each other's guy ropes. Zero machismo. Zero bravado.

References

Deans for Impact (2016). *Practice with Purpose: The Emerging Science of Teacher Expertise*. Austin, TX: Deans for Impact. Available at: https://www.deansforimpact.org/files/assets/practice-with-purpose.pdf.

Drucker, P.F. (1967). 'The effective decision'. *Harvard Business Review*. Available at: https://hbr.org/1967/01/the-effective-decision.

EEF. (2021). 'Effective professional development: guidance report'. Education Endowment Foundation. Available at: https://educationendowmentfoundation.org.uk/education-evidence/guidance-reports/effective-professional-development.

Gov.UK. (2024). 'KS4 performance 2022/23'. Gov.UK. Available at: https://explore-education-statistics.service.gov.uk/find-statistics/key-stage-4-performance.

Keynes, J.M. (1920; digitized 2005). *The Economic Consequences of the Peace*. New York: Harcourt, Brace and Howe.

Ofqual & Stockford, I. (2023). 'Equalities analysis: what the 2023 results tell us'. Gov.UK. Available at: https://www.gov.uk/government/speeches/equalities-analysis-what-the-2023-results-tell-us.

Treadaway, M. (2019). 'Looking within, part 1: How much difference does within-school variation make?'. FFT Education Datalab. Available at: https://ffteducationdatalab.org.uk/2019/03/looking-within-part-1-how-much-difference-does-within-school-variation-make.

Twaronite, K. (2019). 'The surprising power of simply asking coworkers how they're doing'. *Harvard Business Review*. Available at: https://hbr.org/2019/02/the-surprising-power-of-simply-asking-coworkers-how-theyre-doing.

CHAPTER 8
DEVELOPING LEADERS
ISAAC MOORE

Isaac Moore is a deputy headteacher at a 11–18 Academy in Berkshire, England. He leads on curriculum and assessment, staff development and reading. He co-authored *Desirable Difficulties in Action* and speaks regularly at researchED conferences.

To be able to do any of this, school leaders must go about their work in a way that builds relational trust. Robinson (2017) advises that leaders should use 'content knowledge to solve complex school-based problems, while building relational trust with staff, parents, and students'. Relationships and domain-specific knowledge are, therefore, the core themes that will run through this chapter, the focus of which is how to develop leaders. It explores the importance of the environment required to develop leaders, a model for leadership learning, lessons from the EEF evidence review of teacher professional development (Sims et al., 2021), and a proposed framework for leadership development.

Start with a culture of excellence

Bryk et al. (2010) found that for schools to be strong learning environments for students and staff, adults must first work to create a culture of mutual trust and respect. Their work shows the importance of school culture, order and safety in creating an environment where teachers are willing and able to focus on instruction. Analyses by Kraft and Papay (2014) indicate that teachers working in more-supportive professional environments show a greater improvement in effectiveness over time than teachers working in less-supportive environments, listing school culture, order and discipline, and professional development as some of the elements of professional environments.

In poorly run schools, this culture of excellence is lacking and behaviour is often poor. Everything is harder to do in schools like this, as teachers and leaders spend a considerable proportion of their day dealing with the poor behaviour. A head of subject once mentioned to me that to improve her department, she would like to be able to sit down when she is not teaching to have a conversation about the curriculum in terms of what is and isn't working, but that this was almost impossible due to spending most of her time outside her own teaching intervening in poor behaviour in the corridors or removing poorly behaved students from lessons.

It is difficult to develop leaders effectively if this is the kind of environment they work in. Some leaders are still able to work and develop in this kind of school environment, but many will not. To develop all leaders in any school, we must start with a culture that prioritises excellence. In *An Ethic of Excellence*, Ron Berger (2003) identifies five pedagogical principles for creating a culture of excellence. Four of these principles can be applied to developing leaders:

- assign work that matters
- study examples of excellence
- build a culture of critique
- require multiple revisions.

Assigning work that matters is about ensuring that leadership development is focused on the role of leaders; the substance of their work. As part of this development, leaders should be shown models of excellence, given feedback on their development, and supported to become better leaders over time. But there is more to how leaders should learn.

A model of learning for leaders

> Prior domain knowledge is the most important determinant of a student's learning success; ascertain this and teach him accordingly.

> *(Ausubel, 1968)*

The way we should aim to develop leaders follows from how we support students to learn. From decades of research into cognitive science, we know learning takes place by connecting new information to existing knowledge in our long-term memory, that paying attention is the beginning of learning, and that leaders need to be taught and guided to pay attention to the most important signals from the school environment.

As 'memory is the residue of thought' (Willingham, 2009), we therefore learn what we think deeply about. That thinking takes place initially in our working memory. Sense-making happens when the knowledge in our long-term memory acts as a template to figure out the new signal or information. The knowledge that leaders already have in their long-term memory should inform how we go about developing them. Leaders should, therefore, be given time and space to think about the most important knowledge and challenges they face in their roles

We must also be aware of the novice–expert continuum (Sweller et al., 1998) that suggests that how novices learn is very different to how experts learn. Leaders' levels of expertise may differ by domain and school context: one size is not going to fit all. School leadership development needs to recognise this and ensure that developing leadership linked to the core priorities of a school is well planned. There should be a curriculum for leadership development that is sequenced to support knowledge acquisition in specific domains.

Novices have less-organised knowledge (both formal and experience). They, therefore, benefit from being taught sequentially, in small chunks and via explicit instruction (modelling, clear explanation, guided practice). The knowledge of experts is vast in comparison and much more organised, and so they are able to draw on this prior knowledge to solve novel challenges. Novices benefit from the use of scaffolds, which are gradually removed as needed. For example, in a problem-solving task, novice leaders might need to be given steps to follow. Experts, in contrast, will benefit from prior problem-solving and be better able to tackle complex problems without such scaffolds. If we know that the prior knowledge a leader has will determine their ability to develop further, we must find a way to ascertain this. One note of caution: novices may not know what they don't know, and so such new leaders shouldn't be tasked to plan their own professional development. Collaborative planning under the guidance of an expert in the domain is a better way to proceed.

A framework to guide the development of leaders

Leading well in schools at every level requires a great deal of knowledge and expertise, which are developed through a continually improving mental model of leadership. A mental model is a reasoning mechanism that exists as a knowledge structure in long-term memory. It can be called on to assist the models formed in working memory that support reasoning and problem-solving (Johnson-Laird, 1983; Nersessian, 2002).

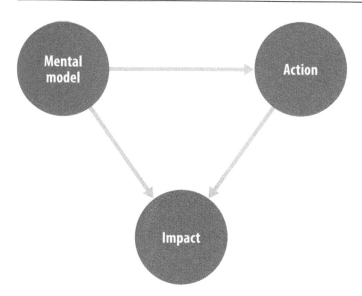

Mental models and expertise (author's own).

Mental models guide our actions and our actions produce impact – positive or negative. But mental models are seldom complete, and there is always a need to regenerate mental models to solve problems. We therefore need to develop leaders' knowledge to make them more effective at tackling the complex and challenging problems that leaders deal with on a daily basis.

Improving the expertise and mental models of leaders can be structured using the IGTP model proposed in the EEF report on the mechanisms of effective professional development (Sims, et al., 2021). The report identifies 14 mechanisms that are put into one of four categories. The four categories are:

- **Insight**: mechanisms in this category include managing cognitive load and revisiting prior knowledge.

- **Goals**: mechanisms in this category include goal setting, using information from a credible source and providing reinforcement after progress.

- **Techniques**: mechanisms in this category include instruction, practical social support, modelling, feedback and rehearsal.

- **Practice**: mechanisms in this category include prompts, action planning, self-monitoring and context-specific repetition

The report concludes that professional development that contains at least one mechanism from each category is three times more likely to have an impact on pupil attainment. If we want our leadership development to be effective, we need to incorporate this into any development programme.

What could a framework for developing school leaders look like?

Osborn et al. (2002) describe leadership development as a 'complex phenomenon' that encompasses the interactions between the leader and the social and organisational environment. Dalakoura (2010) argues that 'leadership practices should provide staff with the opportunity to learn from their work. Leadership development should therefore occur in the context of ongoing work.' As the work that needs to be done will differ by organisation, leadership development is highly context-dependent.

Hrivnak et al. (2009) propose a conceptual framework for designing effective leadership development programmes. They state that their 'objective … is not to outline a specific set of methodologies or instructional tools per se, but rather provide a way to incorporate some modalities in a thoughtful, goal-driven, and comprehensive instructional approach designed to achieve specific, measurable, organisational objectives.' This framework includes:

- beginning with a mutual commitment
- assessing organisational requirements
- conducting gap analysis
- methods of leadership development
- providing feedback
- an emphasis on experiential learning
- assessment of leadership development outcomes.

What type of framework can support the development of leaders in schools? Below, I suggest a framework that can be useful. What the output of using this suggested framework looks like is, again, context-dependent. It takes into consideration the importance of the culture and environment in which leaders work, the core priorities of the school, the competencies of the role, the needs of the individual leader and our latest understanding of the mechanisms of effective professional development. Using leaders with the expertise to support the development of leaders can happen formally (such as on professional development courses) or in line-management meetings. Where a line manager does not have the expertise, the school may need to engage with external professionals with the required expertise. An approach to leadership development in this model is sketched as a flow diagram below.

1. Identify the type of culture and environment that will support all leaders to do their best work.

2. Identify the core priorities of the school that are linked directly to student outcomes.

3. Clearly map out the knowledge that leaders need to have to solve the priority challenges in their roles.

4. Sequence the knowledge so that it becomes incremental over time.

5. Design a professional development programme based on the need of the leader using the four categories and a combination of mechanisms that are effective for the school context.

6. Source professionals with the expertise to support leaders to have the knowledge that they need.

A proposed framework to support the development of leaders in schools (author's own).

Teach leaders how to make good decisions

To think from first principals means to question your assumptions about a problem and build a solution by breaking down these assumptions. These assumptions can sometimes arise as a consequence of incomplete mental models. Schools are very busy places; when faced with a challenge, we turn first to our past experiences or knowledge of what others have done. This is known as reasoning from analogy. Human beings find thinking hard, and most people look for shortcuts. For example, a leader may have solved a past challenge X by doing Y. When the context changes, Y may no longer be a good solution to problem X. The change in context may be moving schools, teaching a different year group or a different teacher being assigned to a teaching group. If our context is different, then what was done in the past or in another school may not be the solution we need now.

The complex challenges leaders face sometimes require them to think about challenges in a new way. Thinking from first principles is a way to ensure clarity and strong decision-making. Your thinking gets better when you question or move away from your assumptions. Some suggested steps to thinking from first principles are:

1. **Define the challenge you want to solve.** For example, if you are faced with the challenge of students not completing homework, you may conclude it is because they are lazy. This leads you down a path that is different from the path you would follow if you found out that the reason was because students are often not successful in lessons.

2. **List your assumptions about the challenge.** Be honest. An assumption could be that a leader thinks they can judge learning by doing a learning walk.

3. **Ask why.** Why do you think you can judge learning from a learning walk? Keeping asking why.

4. **Break the problem down into its critical parts.** If a colleague is teaching a lesson the way that it was co-planned but students are not doing well, try to break down the problem into its parts and look at each part in detail.

5. **Test your solution and gather feedback.** This may be as part of a learning conversation in your line-management meetings.

6. **Implement, review and refine.**

All leaders need practice in making challenging decisions as part of their professional development as these decisions underpin every aspect of change management and school improvement in their remit.

Teach leaders how to have developmental and accountability conversations

One of the key ways we develop leaders is through relationships, often one to one, in line-management meetings. Without effective relationships, we might damage, or at best slow down, the development of leaders. Both challenging poor practice and developing others rely on effective conversations. These can sometimes be difficult, and many leaders avoid them for this reason. Avoiding the conversation or having it in a way that damages relationships will make leaders work in ineffective ways and slow down their development.

One of the ways to ensure that relationships are effective is to teach leaders how to have conversations. Open-to-learning conversations are one way to do this. Robinson (2017) states that 'at the heart of open-to-learning conversations is openness to learning – learning about the quality of the thinking and information that we use when making judgments about what is happening, why and what to do about it.' Open-to-learning conversations are a model of interpersonal effectiveness that can help leaders to support and challenge those they manage. Effective open-to-learning conversations improve the validity of information leaders have, increase respect and secure commitment. Underpinning these conversations is respect, which is important for credibility and building relational trust between colleagues.

How do we engage in open-to-learning conversations?

The steps in an open-to-learning conversation (Robinson, 2017)	An example of how this conversation could go
1. Describe your concern as your point of view.	I am concerned about the quality of teaching taking place in your subject.
2. Describe what your concern is based on.	I did some lesson visits in your subject this week and noticed that the vocabulary that was taught in the different classrooms was not the same even though teachers were teaching the same knowledge.
3. Invite the other's point of view.	Does this sound correct to you? What am I missing?
4. Paraphrase their point of view and check with them.	I am going to summarise the points you have made just to be sure that I have heard you correctly.
5. Detect and check important assumptions.	What made you think that teaching the same vocabulary in different classrooms for the same knowledge is problematic? What is the evidence that supports this position?
6. Establish a common ground.	We both agree that teaching the same knowledge but focusing on different vocabulary in different classrooms may disadvantage some students. We know this is not what we want for our students.
7. Make a plan to achieve what you both want.	In your next co-planning meeting, explain why all teachers need to focus on the same vocabulary when teaching the same knowledge and plan the vocabulary for your next topics.

Reproduced with permission © Professor V.M. Robinson.

In step 2, the leader presents the evidence on which their concern is based. The evidence is not treated as the gospel truth, but as a hypothesis that needs exploring. The leader seeks confirmation or disconfirmation. In step 3, the leader invites the presentation of evidence or an explanation from the colleague, just in case there is something the leader has missed. Step 4 is where the leader further shows that they value the colleague and they have listened carefully to their point of view. Step 5 is an opportunity for both parties to learn together. What are the assumptions that are driving the decisions we make? What is an evidence-based way forward? Establishing a common ground in step 6 is absolutely essential as it creates a feeling of 'us against the challenge' and can therefore lead to collaborative problem solving. Finally, step 7 invites commitment from both parties: it does not matter who comes up with the plan, as long as both parties contribute to it.

Line management and relationships

Where there is relational trust between leaders, there is no limit to the level of challenge and support that is on offer. The purpose of challenge is to develop a leader's domain-specific knowledge (knowledge of the role), the way they think and their decision making. Support will be based on knowledge of the challenges that the leader faces and an understanding of possible solutions to those challenges. Senior leaders become better able to support others by increasing their knowledge of the domain. This challenge-and-support structure is often formalised during line-management meetings.

Line-management meetings are essential to develop leaders, whether senior or middle. These meetings help to align the work of leaders to achieve the core priorities of the school. Over time, they support colleagues to develop their mental models as well as providing a forum for challenge and support. The work of challenging the thinking, decisions and actions of a leader in relation to the core priorities of a school is a vital part of these meetings. Leaders need to be able to do this without fear of damaging the relationship. It is, therefore, important that leaders are taught to have challenging conversations in order to develop their practice.

Returning to the leadership-development framework proposed earlier, collaboratively designing a professional development programme that meets the development needs of a middle leader or senior leader, including any conversations about sourcing experts or courses that meet the needs of the leader, is most likely to take place in line-management meetings. For all these reasons, line-management time should be protected each week.

A case study on leadership of curriculum

1. A curriculum for subject leaders

Two years ago at my school, we wanted to formalise the core knowledge that all subject leaders needed to have to become more effective in their roles and to support their professional development. The following table lists the core knowledge that we decided this curriculum should contain. The sessions on culture, values and behaviour were compulsory for all, but subject leaders could then select other sessions based on their development needs as discussed through line management.

Domain-specific knowledge	A breakdown of the knowledge
Culture, values and behaviours	The artefacts of our core values and deliberate practice Building relational trust Open-to-learning conversations; accountability conversations Instructional coaching Effective subject co-planning/CPD Curriculum conversations with SLT as subject experts
Subject curriculum and teaching	Knowledge structures of subjects What it means to make progress in the subject Model of how we learn Knowledge sequencing Motivating pupils through teaching Literacy and the curriculum Observing lessons
Assessment and data	The four pillars of assessment Assessing learning and the curriculum Making sense of data
Career pathways and further professional development	Becoming an assistant head Becoming a head of department Becoming a pastoral leader

Senior leaders working with subject leaders who are new to role use this to plan the next steps in the development of their colleagues. This planning also involves using graphic organisers to support task-scheduling and decision-making. Task-scheduling helps to ensure that new middle leaders are not overwhelmed. A graphic organiser in the form of a flow chart, an example of which follows, supports decision-making and the leader's development. Please note that this example is school specific and would need to be tailored to fit a different context.

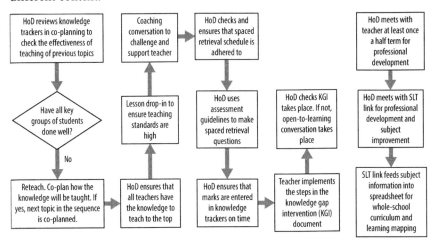

An example of a flowchart for task scheduling for a new head of department.

2. Deep knowledge of the subject curriculum: Subject leaders and SLT link

The relationship between subject leaders and senior leaders is critical in the work that is done on the curriculum and its implementation for impact. Where this relationship is ineffective, the work on the curriculum suffers. Senior leaders need to know enough about the subject to be able to challenge and support in equal measure. So much of successful leadership of subjects rests on leaders' knowledge – of the context, the curriculum and how pupils learn and improve in that specific subject.

One way to enhance the effectiveness of this relationship is through the use of external subject experts to review the curriculum and its implementation. In schools where subject leadership needs development, external subject experts might be supportive of this. Subject reviews are a good starting point for this curriculum conversation because they draw on subject-specific expertise as well as providing an external, objective perspective. They also tend to focus leaders on the core business of the curriculum. What is the purpose of the curriculum? What are the knowledge domains in the subject and what does getting better in each domain look like? Developing subject leadership involves supporting leaders to have the knowledge required to answer these questions.

Other questions that leaders need to understand include the structure and sequencing of subject knowledge. Ideally, a subject review should include an opportunity for the external expert to visit lessons to see how curriculum, pedagogy and assessment interact in the classroom. The curriculum conversation with external subject experts gives senior leaders the opportunity to listen and to try to understand the subject at a deep level. This is essential to building a relationship where there is meaningful challenge that improves subject leaders.

Knowledge guides actions, and effective actions lead to meaningful impact. There is a lot of knowledge in subject communities. To support the development of curriculum leadership, leaders should be encouraged to become active members of subject associations and have regular curriculum conversations with the best minds of the subjects.

3. Development through effective relationships

Nothing happens in schools without curating effective relationships at all levels. In my context, we focus on the relationship between senior leaders and subject leaders and the relationship between subject leaders and class teachers. The first part of the work involved training senior leaders on how to have open-to-learning conversations, as explored above. In subsequent line-management meetings, senior leaders used this format to challenge middle leaders when required. But beyond leaders, we also taught subject leaders how to have these conversations with colleagues within their teams.

We now have a system that requires subject leaders to meet with class teachers at planned, mutually agreed and regular times to have conversations about curriculum implementation, learning and the development of individual teachers. Providing the time for these conversations is so important for building relational trust. Where middle leaders do not yet know how to have these conversations, this forms part of their own professional development first. Relational trust in subject teams improves when teachers feel valued, listened to and respected for their knowledge. These conversations support the development of both subject leaders and teachers.

In summary

- To develop school leaders effectively at every level, a supportive professional environment is needed.
- A supportive professional environment is characterised by a culture of excellence, order and discipline, and professional development.

- The professional development of leaders hinges on the quality of relationships between senior and middle leaders and between middle leaders and class teachers.
- Leaders' mental models of their roles are often incomplete and there is, therefore, a need to deliberately plan for the professional development of leaders as they carry out their roles.
- The way leaders learn is not different from the way students learn. The model of learning from cognitive science should, therefore, be applied to how we develop leaders.
- A leadership-development framework that incorporates some of the 14 mechanisms of effective professional development can be used to develop both novice and expert leaders.
- Leaders need to be taught how to have conversations in a way that builds relational trust. The technique of open-to-learning conversations is one of the ways this can be done.
- Line-management meetings are one of the avenues for developing both senior and middle leaders.

References

Ausubel, D.P. (1968). *Educational Psychology: A Cognitive View*. Holt, Rinehart and Winston: New York.

Berger, R. (2003). *An Ethic of Excellence*. Portsmouth, NH: Heinemann Educational Books.

Bryk, A.S., Bender Sebring, P., Allensworth, E., Luppescu, S. & Easton, J.Q. (2010). *Organizing Schools for Improvement: Lessons from Chicago*. (Kindle version). Chicago & London: The University of Chicago Press.

Dalakoura, A. (2010). 'Differentiating leader and leadership development: A collective framework for leadership development'. *Journal of Management Development*, 29(5), pp.432–441. doi: 10.1108/02621711011039204.

EEF. (2021). 'Effective professional development: guidance report'. Education Endowment Foundation. Available at: https://educationendowmentfoundation. org.uk/education-evidence/guidance-reports/effective-professional-development.

Hrivnak, G.A., Reichard, R.J. & Riggio, R.E. (2009). 'A framework for leadership development'. In S.J. Armstrong & C.V. Fukami (eds) *The SAGE Handbook of Management Learning, Education and Development*, pp.456–475, Sage Publishing.

Johnson-Laird, P.N. (1983). *Mental Models*. Cambridge, UK: Cambridge University Press.

Kraft M.A. & Papay J.P. (2014). 'Can professional environments in schools promote teacher development? Explaining heterogeneity in returns to teaching experience'. *Educational Evaluation and Policy Analysis*, 36(4), pp.476–500. doi: 10.3102/0162373713519496.

Nersessian, N.J. (2002). 'The cognitive basis of model-based reasoning in science'. In P. Carruthers, S. Stich & M. Siegal (eds). *The Cognitive Basis of Science* (pp.133–153), Cambridge, UK: Cambridge University Press.

Osborn, R.N., Hunt, J.G. & Jauch, L.R. (2002). 'Toward a contextual theory of leadership'. *The Leadership Quarterly*, 13(6), pp.797–837.

Rees, T. (2020). '2020: A new perspective for school leadership?' (blog). Ambition Institute. Available at: https://www.ambition.org.uk/blog/2020-new-perspective-school-leadership.

Robinson, V.M. (2017). 'Capabilities required for leading improvement: Challenges for researchers and developers'. Research Conference 2017. Available at: https://research.acer.edu.au/cgi/viewcontent. cgi?article=1306&context=research_conference.

Sims, S., Fletcher-Wood, H., O'Mara-Eves, A., Cottingham, S., Stansfield, C., Van Herwegen, J. & Anders, J. (2021). 'What are the characteristics of effective teacher professional development? A systematic review and meta-analysis'. London: Education Endowment Foundation. Available at: https:// educationendowmentfoundation.org.uk/education-evidence/evidence-reviews/ teacher-professional-development-characteristics.

Sweller, J., van Merrienboer, J.J.G. & Paas, F. (1998). 'Cognitive architecture and instructional design'. *Educational Psychology Review*, [online] 10(3), pp.251–296. doi: 10.1023/a:1022193728205.

Willingham, D.T. (2009). *Why Don't Students Like School?: A Cognitive Scientist Answers Questions About How the Mind Works and What it Means for the Classroom.* San Francisco: Jossey-Bass/John Wiley & Sons.

CHAPTER 9
DEVELOPING TEACHING IN YOUR DEPARTMENT
ADAM ROBBINS

Adam Robbins is a lead practitioner responsible for whole-school CPD in a large coastal comprehensive school. He was a head of science for 7 years and, as such, has a keen interest in how middle leaders can drive teacher improvement. Adam is the author of Middle Leadership Mastery and runs courses and workshops on effective middle leadership both in the UK and abroad. Adam blogs at adam-robbins.com.

Recent years have seen a welcome shift from having professional development run centrally in schools, to allowing departments to have more time to develop their teaching at a more subject-specific level. This has created an accompanying shift in the role of middle leaders, specifically heads of department (HoDs), from a role predominantly focused on administrative support to one that is focused on developing teaching and quality assurance.

Yet the administrative elements of the role have not been subsumed elsewhere, so it is probably no surprise that many HoDs find themselves having to plan regular department sessions that must balance the logistical needs of the team as well as prioritising the team's development as teachers. We'll look at some of the mitigations for the time challenge later in this chapter, but first we'll consider how HoDs might go about planning the professional development of their teachers.

Identifying the areas of focus

Before HoDs begin to look at planning department CPD sessions, it is critical to first identify priorities. Unfortunately, we will never have the time to work on all areas of teaching; we must prioritise the most important areas. To identify these, we can use a broad range of evidence. We can visit lessons and look in books to see what routines and techniques are effective. For example, in some lessons, a HoD might see effective routines and good subject knowledge; in other lessons, they might witness gaps in subject knowledge, poor routines or a lack of responsive teaching. In books, a HoD might look to compare curriculum coverage between classes and teachers, or look for evidence of students working independently and improving their work based on teacher feedback. Common areas of development noted in these observations might point towards potential foci for the next departmental development goal.

In some subjects, HoDs can analyse students' performance in internal and external assessments to identify possible areas of focus within their team. This might reveal consistent areas of poor performance within one individual teacher's class indicating personal areas for teacher improvement, or it might indicate cohort-level gaps in how effectively a particular aspect of the course is being taught across the department. Another option to identify a focus area is to survey teachers to see what their own opinions of their teaching are. We should, however, be cautious in how much weight we attribute to this: self-evaluation is notoriously difficult given the broad range of expertise within the average department (Kruger & Dunning, 1999).

A good way of looking at the areas to prioritise is to break them into two broad categories:

1. **Subject knowledge**: the knowledge of the curriculum content that is being taught.

2. **Pedagogical content knowledge**: the knowledge of what approaches and techniques are involved to teach this subject knowledge well.

In any department, one might present itself as more of a priority than the other. Staff might be very clear on areas of subject knowledge they feel less secure in, but the pedagogical content knowledge might be less clear. For example, a science teacher might very easily accept that they are not a subject specialist in physics so need to develop their knowledge in the subject, but find it harder to see the gaps in their own teaching. There might even be genuine debate on how best to teach certain concepts: in science, for example, some teachers subscribe to a discovery-based practical approach to teaching the subject whereas others believe a more explicit instruction approach is more effective, and so the combined pedagogical content knowledge of the department requires aligning before it can be developed.

It is, therefore, vital that a HoD has a clear vision of what they think great teaching in their subject looks like. They will need to have expertise in evidence-informed pedagogical content knowledge as well as subject knowledge. Furthermore, their subject-level understanding then needs to be compatible with the whole school's vision for teaching and learning to ensure pupils are benefiting from a consistent teaching approach across the school. The

HoD's vision of great teaching must also bear in mind the local context of the school's intake and how best to serve pupils' needs.

We could think of the vision of teaching to be constructed as in the following diagram.

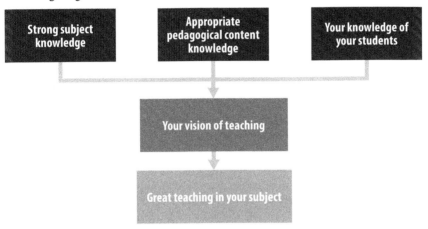

How the vision of teaching in your subject is constructed (author's own).

Planning your priorities

With a clear vision of teaching established and data gathered, key priorities can be identified for the coming term or year. Now it is time to consider planning these priorities into the available department time. In each school, the time available to meet will be varied, so HoDs must choose carefully how best to spend their time. Here are some areas HoDs might be mindful of when doing this:

- **Recognise that CPD is important but not urgent.** This means that it can sometimes be pushed to the side in favour of urgent logistical work. HoDs should fight to avoid this instinct. Middle leaders will often spend their time working week to week, completing urgent tasks for their line managers to ensure the school's overall operations run smoothly. Unfortunately, this can take up a lot of their time and so things that appear less immediately urgent, like planning a CPD session, get pushed back and end up being rushed (if they happen at all), leading to unstructured sessions with key aspects, like embedding into practice or well-chosen examples and scenarios, missing.

- **Pre-plan meetings that will be required to focus solely on logistical issues.** Things like moderation, standardisation and preparing for open evenings will need some protected time for teachers to conduct them effectively, so time must be set aside for them.

- **In meetings, try to avoid spending time on notices and updates.** Save these for email or bulletins. Protect the time available for CPD as much as possible. A good rule of thumb is to save face-to-face time for things that can only be successfully completed when face to face.

Having established the priorities, we can begin to map out when we might want to cover each of them. It is natural to think with a heuristic of 'CPD session done = Job done', and to plan in week 1 to hit our first priority, week 2 the second and so on. If only it was that simple. As educators, we need to plan for habits to be formed. It might be completely reasonable to spend an entire term focusing on introducing and embedding a single complex priority, such as checking for understanding or effective explanations. Other things might be covered sufficiently in a handful of sessions, for example supervision of independent work or routines for effective lesson starts. Either way, your plan will need to be flexible, and it is important to find time to revisit and embed habits in subsequent sessions and during lesson visit feedback.

Finding time to get things done

For most middle leaders, the difference between the priorities you have and the time available is significant. One of the best ways to try to alleviate this time crunch is what I call 'twin objectives', which essentially means seeing each department CPD session as an opportunity to address two things simultaneously.

The first will be subject knowledge. By looking at the curriculum teachers are preparing to deliver, we can identify an area of subject knowledge that we can review and explore teachers' understanding of. Essentially: 'What are we teaching?' The second objective can be a pedagogical-content knowledge objective: a focus on a particular classroom technique. This could be a routine, a questioning approach or anything that might answer the question, 'How is this subject taught best?'.

By putting the two together we can ensure that even teachers with the strongest subject knowledge benefit from improving their pedagogy, and so both objectives address our priorities and ensure that teachers' time is well spent.

These dual objectives, that follow from our departmental information gathering, provide a context to build our training around and also ground any practice or co-planning we try to do to embed the new ideas. It could look something like the following figure.

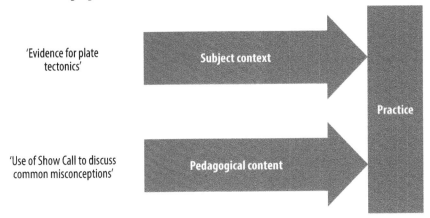

Time can be saved by using a CPD session to address twin objectives, one subject based, the other pedagogical (author's own).

How to structure a department CPD session

With the outline in place and priorities identified, it is time to consider the structure of the sessions themselves.

The EEF has outlined 14 mechanisms essential for effective CPD for educators, grouped into four broad categories: Building knowledge, Motivating teachers, Developing teacher techniques, and Embedding practice (EEF, 2021; Meols Cop Research School, 2021). Below is a quick summary of the mechanisms within each category:

1. **Building knowledge**

   • Revisit prior learning: Revisiting core principles and practices from previous training programmes to reinforce learning and build on existing knowledge.

2. **Motivating teachers**

   • Credible sources of information: Providing an evidence-based rationale and research sources to support the adopted approaches and methodologies, ensuring teachers understand the evidence behind them.

- Setting and agreeing goals: Establishing clear objectives and mutually agreeing on objectives, making the professional growth structured and goal-oriented.

3. **Developing teacher techniques**

- Instructing teachers on how to perform a technique: Offering clear guidance, modelling and resources to staff on specific techniques, breaking down strategies into manageable chunks for better understanding and implementation.
- Arranging social support: Facilitating peer discussion, feedback and coaching to support teachers in refining their techniques and strategies.
- Modelling the technique: Using live demonstrations and video examples to model desired strategies and techniques.
- Rehearsing the technique: Encouraging teachers to practice new techniques, either among peers or in their respective subject areas, to reinforce learning and improve proficiency.

4. **Embedding practice**

- Providing prompts and cues: Regularly reminding teachers about new practices to foster their incorporation into daily routines.
- Prompting action planning: After each training session, encouraging reflection and action planning for teachers to continue refining and implementing new techniques.
- Prompting context-specific repetition: Offering opportunities for departments to adapt and embed new practices within their specific contexts, promoting discussion and collaboration.

Reading this list, it is likely you will be thinking to yourself: 'this list has a lot of things in common with good teaching'. Humans learn in much the same way no matter what their age; the key difference is the level of expertise and prior knowledge a teacher has compared with a student. This will affect some of the choices we make, as experts thrive more from problem-solving than novices do (Kalyuga et al., 2011). It is important, however, to remember that expertise is context-specific: an experienced teacher might have great expertise in the subject knowledge you are using, but be a relative novice in some areas of pedagogical-content knowledge.

This is where our planning of a session should start: by considering what prior knowledge our team might have. If this is activated at the start of the session, it will be easier to build on existing knowledge.

We then need to motivate the team. CPD often involves teachers having to stop doing something and replace it with a new strategy. The original practice might already be pretty good, or something they have come to rely on in lessons. This can be motivationally complex, so it is vital we get them on side. The most effective way to do this is to frame the session as the solution to a persistent problem.

Mary Kennedy's work on persistent problems in teacher training revolves around the fundamental challenges teachers encounter within the classroom environment (Kennedy, 2016). Below is a breakdown of the key components derived from her work.

Kennedy developed a framework identifying common challenges that teachers face, which is not specific to any subject, grade or context, emphasising the intrinsic nature of teaching as a complex and dynamic practice.

Identified persistent problems

- **Portraying the curriculum**: Making the subject's domain knowledge accessible and memorable to students through planning, sequencing and resourcing lessons.
- **Managing student behaviour**: Making sure the classroom environment is safe and productive.
- **Enlisting student participation**: Ensuring students are all thinking hard about the right things and participating.
- **Coping with diversity**: Addressing and adapting to the various needs, backgrounds and abilities of students.
- **Exposing student thinking**: Evaluating students' understanding and retention of the material so we can support their next steps in learning.

We are more likely to activate teachers' motivation if we pitch our session as a potential solution to a persistent problem they commonly face. For example, a session on checking for understanding might start with framing the session around the problem of setting up independent work and then discovering that some students are unable to begin due to poor understanding of the task or concepts.

By now we have activated the relevant prior knowledge, either by revisiting some key facts, perhaps through quizzing, or by asking the team to reflect on their current practice around a strategy or topic. We have set the stage and the team know what we are doing in the session and why.

Next, we need to deliver the new practice or knowledge. It might be that the HoD is best placed to deliver, however it could be better for an expert to step in. If it is another colleague, the session may need to be delayed to allow time for them to do some preparation ahead of delivering.

How, in the session, is it best to explain this change? Should we live model it, discuss and agree on a consensus? Troubleshoot a few suggestions? Watch a video from a webinar? This is where context comes into play. We need to ensure that whoever is delivering the session is either credible or using ideas and practice from a credible source. We want to make sure our team know that time and consideration have gone into recommending this strategy. This could mean we get a member of our team who has demonstrated great skill in the areas being covered, a non-specialist expert in a particular area such as SEND or a team leader who has been researching the work of a well-respected practitioner.

When we deliver training to our teachers, we need to embody the approach that works with our students. We need to break our explanation down into small chunks and use plenty of examples as well as non-examples. Examples are critical to ensure teachers are not just aware of how to do this but also when to do it and, crucially, when and how *not* to do it. Non-examples will support staff to understand the mistakes teachers might make when employing this method or technique and how to avoid them. This is sometimes known as the applicability and utility conditions of an idea (Reif, 2010). We also need to check for understanding to make sure our intended message is the one that is received.

The next stage is often the hardest: implementation in current practice. Up until this point, we have not established any change in our teachers. They have an increased awareness, but without time and effort spent embedding this new knowledge they will struggle to bridge the gap between knowing the strategy and using the strategy.

Embedding into practice is often rushed. We have five minutes left of the session so it becomes a quick 'turn to someone and discuss how you will use this in a lesson next week'. Instead, we need to consider and plan the embedding phase carefully. It does not have to come directly after the others, so if more time is needed, the first meeting could be mainly delivering new ideas while a later, follow-up meeting revisits this and spends time focusing on embedding the ideas into practice. This is not ideal, but it is pragmatic.

There are many approaches to embedding a new strategy. Some favour a deliberate practice model, where pairs or groups of teachers rehearse a strategy in an empty classroom. There are studies that have demonstrated that deliberate practice is an effective tool for teacher development (Grant, 2022). Grant's systematic review of the literature and research to date found that, on the whole, teachers learned more from deliberate practice activities and went on to make changes more readily. These highly structured sessions aim to support teachers in working on a particular area for development with expert colleagues providing instantaneous feedback on their performance (Ericsson et al., 1993). The opportunity for rehearsal allows teachers to avoid the possibility of failing in front of a live class of pupils, and prepares them to be more confident in delivering to the class.

That said, not all aspects of teaching lend themselves easily to the kind of deliberate practice we often think of, such as rehearsing a teaching technique. Just like task design for students, the embedding phase of a CPD session needs to focus on encouraging teachers to think carefully about the strategies introduced. Co-planning and sharing ideas might be another effective mode of consolidation, as might adapting classroom resources. Discussing scenarios as a team can be an effective way to help teachers embed new ideas into their practice, provided they are well chosen to illustrate the applicability conditions of an idea effectively. We need to make it clear to our teams what successful implementation looks like and what benefits they might expect. By allowing them to practice, action plan and visualise success, colleagues can monitor and reflect on their own progress. This can become a shared focus over the week, feeding into any informal discussion or quality assurance systems such as learning walks.

In busy schools, there will always be a tension between the amount of time available and the time needed to ensure sufficient practice. While it is impossible to say exactly how much time an individual teacher will need to practice, my personal rule of thumb is to think how much time you think you will need and double it. Once there has been sufficient time to practice, it is appropriate to bring the group back together to reflect. This is a good opportunity to get the team to feed back on what has been delivered, to check their understanding, to address any concerns or queries that have arisen in the embedding phase, and to agree next steps. This also allows time to discuss the support that teachers might need to help them adapt, put it in place in advance and ensure success. The team can use this time to record their personal reflections and commit to using the technique. If it is a big change then it might be beneficial to shrink this change by having them focus on using it with a single class. Reflection goes both ways, so it is useful for the deliverer to reflect and welcome any feedback on how the session was delivered. This allows them to improve their own practice and model being the reflective practitioner we wish all teachers to be.

The following table summarises this approach and offers some prompt questions for each phase.

Aspect of the session	Questions to consider
Do Now Ensure that the 'Do Now' is presented when participants enter the room	• What existing knowledge do my team have? • What knowledge needs to be recalled and built on in this session?
Set the scene (motivating staff)	• Key question to address today • Why is this the focus? • What is the challenge this will overcome? (isn't it annoying when . . .) • Is there anything we are already doing well that is contributing towards overcoming this challenge?
Deliver the new ideas	• Who will explain this and how? • Who will model this and how? • What credible source are you drawing the new ideas from? • How will you manage cognitive load of colleagues?
Embedding into practice	• How much time will be given to deliberate practice within the session? • What is the best way to practise this idea? Does it need deliberate practice in pairs? Or will co-planning provide more appropriate cues and support? • What cues will you give staff to use to help build a new habit?
Reflect on the session and commit to the next steps to embed learning into practice	• Set and agree on goals/actions to take following this session. • How will participants be supported to embed this practice, for example, co-planning, learning walks, joint reflection? • What does success look like following this session? • Reflections for presenter: How will we know this is being embedded? Who will offer you feedback on your delivery of the session?

What if I never get enough department time?

If you are unable to create time for regular CPD with your team but recognise its importance, you find yourself in a frustrating situation. There is a potential solution that might help provide some of the CPD you need in a very short timeframe. I call it micro-CPD.

Micro-CPD is a rolling model of CPD that aims to fit into just 15 minutes a week. Hopefully, staff will be willing to commit to attending this on top of their directed hours and outside their normal meetings.

Because it is so short, it needs to be simple. We must sacrifice some of the mechanisms of effective CPD but, due to its regularity, these mechanisms will build over time with most being covered as the sessions develop. It is worth remembering at this stage that while the mechanisms outlined in the EEF (2021) report are advantageous, it should not be seen as an all-or-nothing list. These sessions follow a very simple process.

Firstly, agree a theme. This will be your priority for a long time, so make sure you choose the one you think will have the greatest impact on your team when you consider their current strengths and areas for development.

Each session has three phases, each lasting just five minutes:

1. **Reflect on the last session**: As teachers enter, there might be a few prompt questions ready for them. Teachers are encouraged to use these to discuss how things have gone over the last week. If this is the first session, these questions frame the persistent problem to be tackled in the session.

2. **New input**: Five minutes of new information. This is a small chunk, not the whole idea rushed; maybe just the first step.

3. **Reflect and commit**: A five-minute discussion and feedback, with any questions answered and space for teachers to try the idea out.

This process repeats each week with the idea that, over a series of weeks, teachers will understand more and have opportunities to practise the new technique and develop their teaching. As there is regular review, the idea stays live in team members' minds and is often a point of more casual discussion outside these 15-minute sessions. This creates a high level of social support that helps the idea to embed.

To conclude, department CPD is a challenging and rewarding part of modern subject leadership. By carefully planning and delivering sessions, we can greatly improve the quality of education our students receive.

References

Education Endowment Foundation (2021). 'Effective professional development: guidance report'. Education Endowment Foundation. Available at: https://educationendowmentfoundation.org.uk/education-evidence/guidance-reports/effective-professional-development.

Ericsson, K.A., Krampe, R.T. & Tesch-Römer, C. (1993). 'The role of deliberate practice in the acquisition of expert performance'. *Psychological Review*, 100(3), pp.363–406.

Grant, D.G. (2022). 'Becoming an expert on purpose: How deliberate practice informs teacher effectiveness'. In H. Şenol (ed.) *Pedagogy – Challenges, Recent Advances, New Perspectives, and Applications*. London: IntechOpen Ltd.

Kalyuga, S., Ayres, P., Chandler, P. & Sweller, J. (2011). 'The expertise reversal effect'. *Educational Psychologist*, 38(1), pp.23–31. doi: 10.1007/978-1-4419-8126-4_12.

Kennedy, M. (2016). 'Parsing the practice of teaching'. *Journal of Teacher Education*, 67(1), pp.6–17.

Kruger, J. & Dunning, D. (1999). 'Unskilled and unaware of it: How difficulties in recognizing one's own incompetence lead to inflated self-assessments'. *Journal of Personality and Social Psychology*, 77(6), pp.1121–1134.

Meols Cop Research School. (2021). 'Design and deliver effective professional development'. Available at: https://researchschool.org.uk/meolscop/news/design-and-deliver-effective-professional-development.

Reif, F. (2010). *Applying Cognitive Science to Education: Thinking and Learning in Scientific and Other Complex Domains*. Cambridge, MA: The MIT Press.

CHAPTER 10
WHAT DOES IT MEAN TO LEAD PROFESSIONAL DEVELOPMENT ACROSS A TRUST?
JON GILBERT

Jon Gilbert is the Professional Learning and Improvement Director for The Two Counties Trust, a trust of secondary schools in Nottinghamshire and Derbyshire. In this role, Jon heads the trust's Professional Learning Academy and works with schools in the trust to provide the very best professional learning for all staff in the organisation. Jon is also the Lead Facilitator for Deliberate Practice for the National Institute of Teaching. Jon has been a teacher of RE and sociology, a head of department and a senior leader, working in high-performing schools in areas of high disadvantage in Bradford and Leeds.

For years, when my young daughter was asked what her daddy did for a living, she would proudly respond, 'He is a teacher'. Easy peasy. Everyone knows what that means. Now she is less sure what to say. Her daddy is in fact the Professional Learning and Improvement Director at The Two Counties Trust. Leading professional development (PD) across a multi-academy trust (MAT) is a much-less-clearly-defined role. In fact, it is a role that is constantly evolving within the English education system and is rather nuanced depending on context and experience. In this chapter, I will seek to provide some clarity on what it means to lead PD across a trust. I will begin with a history of the development of this kind of trust-wide role, then I will delve into some of the nuances of the role, before finally exploring the challenges and opportunities that leading PD across a trust brings. All the more reason for my daughter to double her efforts in learning to read fluently!

Trust professional development: A short history

The origins of trust PD can be associated with two movements. Firstly, the school-led system of school improvement: schools working in networks, federations, local partnerships or, more formally, as teaching schools to support each other and provide PD. In many cases, the schools leading this movement went on to lead MATs and so the role of PD lead in those schools led, naturally, to a role working across a MAT.

The second movement, and one linked to government policy, is the expansion of academies. The earliest MATs were established as a result of the sponsored academies programme, that began in 2002 (Male, 2022; Hatton, Hampson & Drake, 2019; House of Commons Education Committee, 2017), whereby underperforming schools were transferred into MATs to support school improvement. As a result, the earliest trust leaders of PD were often those from high-performing schools working to support those with poorer track records.

Since the Conservative–Liberal Democrat coalition government introduced legislation in 2010 enabling all schools to become academies, there has been a significant increase in the number of both academies and MATs (DfE, 2015). In the five-year period between January 2010 and January 2015 alone, there was an increase from 202 to 4722 academies (Haves, 2022). Similar levels of growth have been seen in MATs: in March 2011 there were 391 MATs, whereas by 2021 there were 1170 (BESA, 2021). As trusts began to grow, not just as a result of underperforming schools being transferred into a MAT but through schools choosing to join MATs, the role of trust PD lead has evolved to support the need for trusts to create clarity and coherence of identity and ways of working, to encourage their growth.

At the time of writing, the government continues to promote a trust-led education system, having set out plans for all schools to be part of a 'strong' trust by 2030 in its 'Opportunity for all' white paper (DfE, 2022a). Drawing on the advantages of scale and reach, the white paper asserts that strong trusts raise educational standards and accelerate school improvement. Given the increasing body of evidence pointing towards the impact high-quality PD can have on student outcomes (EEF, 2021), it is no surprise that effective leadership of consistent, high-quality PD is highlighted as a key facet of a 'strong' trust (DfE, 2022b). This is a sentiment echoed in the codification of strong trusts by the Confederation of School Trusts (CST, 2022). It is natural, then, that many trusts are seeking to harness the potential impact of high-quality PD through establishing posts with responsibility for ensuring this happens.

In 2019, Ofsted published its investigation into MATs titled 'Multi-academy trusts: benefits, challenges and functions' (Ofsted, 2019). The investigation highlights a number of benefits of being part of a MAT. These include back-office support, economies of scale, challenge and support, collaboration and sharing of expertise, and career development and promotion. Like other central roles in a trust, the PD leader has a role to play in realising these benefits.

From supporting the development of administrative and support staff, to talent management, to leading trust-wide subject networks, to delivering cost-effective trust conferences, the role of PD lead has evolved significantly.

The rapid growth in the number of trust PD leads and the variety and evolving nature of their remits is neatly illustrated by a community of trust PD leads that exists on X (formerly Twitter). The group, established in 2022, went from a few like-minded colleagues wanting a sounding board to over 100 trust PD leads in the space of a single year. Tracy Goodyear, Director of Teacher Development at The Mercian Trust and leader of the network, explains more:

> Whilst well-established networks of domain-specific support exist for teachers and senior leaders, when starting my trust-wide role I was conscious that I didn't know anybody who did my job: it was time to build a tribe! The Trust-wide CPD Leaders' Forum was formed in October 2022, with just four members in attendance. What was clear in these early interactions, and what became more evident as this group continued to grow, was that the role of leading professional development at scale held a range of guises, depending on the 'age and stage' of multi-academy trust and the perceived needs within the trust. As a result of this, a series of operating models of this work have emerged – for some leading this work at scale, their roles focus primarily on the delivery of professional development (delivering NPQs/ECF or trust-wide or in-house programmes), for others, their roles were more closely aligned with their trust-wide people strategy, focusing more on HR, recruitment and retention. For others, they serve and support senior leaders and middle leaders in their schools. These wide-ranging and diverse iterations of the role make our community fertile ground for new learning and an ideal forum for exploring possibilities within the trust sector. Whilst the guises of this role are wide-ranging, the core purpose of our members' work remains to serve pupils, schools and staff in improving life chances and outcomes for young people.

Trust professional development: How does it work?

Overall, it is clear that the MAT leader of PD has a role to play in improving the quality of education within their trust through ensuring that colleagues have access to high-quality PD, while also helping to ensure that the plethora of benefits of being part of a trust are realised. But how exactly is this done? What follows will begin to break down the multi-faceted nature of the role of a trust leader of PD and draw on the experiences of those within the role to elucidate what it means to lead PD across a trust. Please note that while I have broken the role down into distinct activities, in reality a PD lead may perform many of these activities in their role simultaneously. Similarly, what I include below does not represent an exhaustive list!

The Deliverer

To ensure colleagues within their trust are accessing high-quality PD opportunities, some trust PD leads spend a significant portion of their time preparing for and delivering training. They may be relied upon to go into schools to deliver training to staff, lead online training or provide training for schools to deliver. Here Dr Chris Baker, Professional Development Lead for the Cabot Learning Federation, explains what this looks like in reality:

> PD delivery is an integral part of my responsibilities across the 35 schools in the Cabot Learning Federation and I feel that our systematic approach to that delivery provides a range of benefits to staff, academies and myself. We leverage our central frameworks for leadership, teaching and learning, and coaching as tools for analysing PD needs, and as a menu of available support. PD leaders commission this tailored support through our termly 1:1 meetings, which provide an opportunity to explore the rationale, logistics, and contextual specificity of the PD request. Beyond the obvious benefits to staff in terms of additional support, PD delivery serves as an excellent opportunity for me to model effective session design and delivery for my in-school PD leads. Delivery also plays a crucial role in maintaining my visibility and credibility across the trust, fostering relationships, and opening doors for further engagement and support. A unique advantage I bring to delivery as trust PD lead is my ability to provide contextual examples from across the trust to enhance the training. Sharing case studies of different application models or highlighting specific examples of excellence is always well-received and facilitates further collaboration and peer problem-solving. In conclusion, it is important to acknowledge the reality of expertise boundaries for trust PD leads seeking to take on the Deliverer role. As you will see in later case studies, when PD requests fall outside my area of expertise, I transition into a Fixer role and seek expert delivery from other staff within the trust or, if necessary, from external sources.

The Fixer

The world of PD is a rather complex one. There is no shortage of organisations and individuals offering PD to schools and trusts, not to mention the seemingly constant stream of education books, blogs and webinars. One key role for a trust leader of PD is to distil all of that noise, forge partnerships with key providers and source 'experts' to deliver PD. Here Sam Gibbs, Trust Lead for Curriculum and Development at the Greater Manchester Education Trust, describes how that is a core feature of her role:

Of equal importance to recognising where your own expertise adds value is the ability to identify and establish relationships with credible partners who can maximise the impact of professional learning. There is certainly no shortage of opportunity, but it is crucial to avoid a scattergun approach – the danger lies in trying to involve too many external people too soon, and implementing too many things at once. Value for money is also an important consideration.

At the Greater Manchester Education Trust, it has been a conscious decision to work with carefully selected partner organisations whose values align with our own, and who can support improvement work around our trust and individual schools' priorities. The benefit of having someone leading this work across a family of schools is their ability to hold the strategic 'big picture'; understanding how the different pieces of the CPD jigsaw fit together so nothing is seen as separate or an 'add-on'.

We have developed four key partnerships, each with a clearly defined purpose. Some benefit all staff directly – we have recently taken out group membership with the Chartered College of Teaching, for example – while others are more indirect, such as our membership of Flourishing Trusts, which brings trust leaders together through collaborative networks. Our relationship with an online platform which supports our coaching, mentoring and CPD is helping us to build a culture of reflective practice across our schools. Finally, it is important that the person leading CPD across a group of schools is able to engage in their own professional learning – for me, the Forum Strategy and the Trust CPD Leaders' Network have been crucial to enable me to forge connections with others in similar roles and consequently provide a higher-quality offer to our staff.

The Facilitator

Some PD leads orchestrate networks of colleagues across their trust, facilitating developmental collaboration and the sharing of best practice. This could be done by bringing together subject networks for regular meetings, organising domain-specific conferences, online events and so on. Here Cat Rushton, Director of ATT (Academy Transformation Trust) Institute, describes how she acts as the Facilitator in her trust:

As a leader of PD in a large, geographically spread MAT it has been my priority to provide frequent, meaningful opportunities for colleagues to collaborate across settings. I achieved this by designing and establishing a network structure of Leadership, Curriculum and Specialist Communities which provide the forum for colleagues with common responsibilities to work on shared priorities.

Ensuring regular meetings is a significant challenge for busy colleagues who have a range of time pressures. Therefore, I ensure community meetings are scheduled in advance, for the whole academic year. We use a predetermined combination of face-face, hybrid and online meetings to ensure the benefits of different mediums are utilised. For example, our curriculum communities meet online five times a year with a scope which is tailored to their developmental needs. This may include curriculum development, working on assessment/moderation, team leadership, results analysis, and so on.

To ensure the most appropriate community members from each academy are identified I created a 'person specification' for each community. These are shared with principals to support selecting members at academy level. From the community members, community leads are identified for their expertise and commitment to continued development. Training for community leads is a significant factor in their and their school's success and I deliver training on the theory of 'Communities of practice' (Webber, 2016), orchestrating successful developmental collaboration, alongside the practicalities of our face-face, online and hybrid meetings.

To support the development of a community culture where colleagues can collaborate effectively and honestly, I created the 'Communities the ATT Way' framework which outlines common values and expected behaviours. This framework is relaunched annually with all community members and our 'Ways of working' are shared by community leads at the start of each meeting.

Finally, and most importantly, it is essential the work of our communities positively impacts the experience of learners in our academies. I ensure this by providing guidance to community members on how to contextualise the priorities of their community and feed back to SLT. By continually reinforcing the role that community members play in academy improvement I ensure feedback is welcomed by senior leaders. Importantly, each of our academies has a professional development lead, a member of the professional development community, which I am privileged to lead. The role of these colleagues is pivotal in assimilating feedback from every community member to ensure academies implement the products and decisions made in communities sensitively and sustainably.

The Knowledge Architect

We know that teacher skill without knowledge and understanding can lead to poor decision-making in the classroom, blind imitation or misapplication of strategies. Building knowledge is crucial in developing an informed, empowered workforce, with sensitivity to nuance of phase, subject, context and individual children. Trust PD leads are increasingly architects of PD curriculum design. They collate or signpost, sequencing and cohering knowledge and opportunities to build and embed skills around areas of need for their teams. Trust PD leads do not need to be experts in all fields but can promote and facilitate knowledge-building by individuals and in teams. Knowledge-building takes many tangible forms including trust-wide pedagogy guides and playlists, teach–meet style events, formal training programmes, study groups and blog sharing. Here Judith Kidd, Director of Dixons Centre for Growth, and Mark Miller, Director of Bradford Research School, explain what this looks like in their trust:

Dixons Centre for Growth works to support the professional growth of all teachers in Dixons Academies Trust and beyond, through our work as Bradford Research School. A key aspect of this work is to curate, codify and communicate the best of what we know. Since our early inception as a team of three part-time teachers and leaders working in PD, Initial Teacher Education [ITE] and our research school, we have critically reviewed and synthesised research on topics such as curriculum design, coaching, mentoring, attendance and psychological safety. These are supported by well-chosen bibliographies and mechanisms for debate such as our cross cutting teams. Knowledge is shared to inform discussion and strengthen teacher understanding and implementation. We value and model evidence-literacy and try to ensure that our curation and interpretation are balanced and well-founded.

Acknowledging that busy teachers appreciate the availability of accessible summaries and bitesize videos or blogs, we also know that some want to go further. We provide opportunity and mentoring for teachers with particular interest in academic research and writing and allow groups to be briefed and supported in informed discussion. We provide opportunities to develop research literacy and rich knowledge in our staff through collective sprints and knowledge-building roles such as evidence leads. It is important to us to develop institutional knowledge that is not held by a sole expert but is evident in our artefacts, communication and daily behaviours.

The Knower (and Don't Knower)

Many trust leads for PD have experience of successfully directing staff development as a leader in a school. As such, while a trust lead for Maths is seen as the domain expert in Maths, or the trust lead for English is seen as the go-to person for advice and guidance on all things English, the trust lead for PD is a domain specialist in professional development. A trust-wide leader of PD may be relied upon to bring their knowledge of professional development per se to advise individual schools or the trust as a whole on how best to approach PD in a given situation for teaching and non-teaching staff. If they don't know something, then they probably know a person that would! Similarly, they use their knowledge of the landscape of PD opportunities to leverage these for the benefit of their whole trust and beyond. Tammy Elward, Director of the Spencer Teaching School Hub and Director of the Derby Research School, explains how this works in her trust:

> I play a part in a system, a cog in a wider infrastructure to ensure that the schools we work with get the knowledge and information they need to make the best decisions for their context. This stems from the culture within our trust – we were amongst the first hundred schools designated a Teaching School Alliance and a pathfinder Maths Hub, and so we shared a firm belief in the school-led system. The expertise within and across schools should be mobilised to empower teachers and leaders to be the best they can for their pupils. As the school-led system has matured with more hubs and research schools, more levers for national change such as the National Professional Qualifications (NPQs) and Early Career Framework, so too has our purpose. We serve our immediate family of schools as a trust, but also many hundreds more across our geographical area as advocates of evidence-informed practice, high-quality CPD, and connectivity across the system. So now, my role feels very different: to help schools make sense of what's around them, scan the horizon and judiciously select what serves them best.

> I lead a team of system leaders committed to supporting the Golden Thread – offering staff development from initial teacher training through to the full suite of NPQs and apprenticeships. We aim to help schools navigate the rich opportunities on the landscape and translate it into purposeful action for their settings, to support leadership to improve teaching and learning and impact on pupils. We aim to do

it the best we can so that our core purpose is always held in mind: we serve schools so that they can do the best for their pupils.

The Talent Mapper

As cited above, one of the benefits of being part of a trust is the opportunities it provides for career development. As such, it is part of the remit of many trust PD leads to support a talent-management strategy designed to enable the career progression of staff within the trust. This may start at the beginning of someone's career in education, with the trust PD lead overseeing the trust's Initial Teacher Training (ITT) and Early Careers Framework offers. It may also involve the trust PD lead having oversight of NPQs undertaken by colleagues within the trust (DfE, 2022c). Similarly, it may involve the PD lead developing in-house courses for teaching and non-teaching staff to support their career development. Sufian Sadiq, Director of Teaching School at Chiltern Learning Trust, gives an insight into how that works in his trust:

> The educational, technological and sociological landscape has changed significantly in the past 20 years. The reduced number of teachers in the system creates higher demand due to lower supply. People are inundated with offers via websites, social media and apps for jobs. The cost-of-living crisis means that despite getting it right with organisational culture and wellbeing, staff are still leaving for progression, which can equate to more money and time.

> This presents the opportunity for MATs to centrally view it as one 'eco-system', where we are creating individual and unique roadmaps for staff progression and development. We aim for early identification of exceptional talent, working closely with ITT providers. This encompasses ECT [Early Career Teacher] identification of those demonstrating high-quality teaching and pedagogy, as well as leadership. We focus then on identifying middle leaders, with capabilities for senior leadership, and then senior leaders, capable of headship.

> Once you know the talent, it is about making sure you are aware of their skillset, strengths and areas for development. Nurturing talent is crucial, as sitting back to watch people grow doesn't always end with individuals fulfilling their potential. Providing frameworks for growth, ensuring leaders around them are investing in them and, most importantly perhaps, they know you have spotted them. This is where we invest in ensuring they access professional development. Our professional development is a combination of both accredited qualifications and bespoke internal courses designed to provide practical leadership insights.

Sometimes you have individuals sat there on the 'bench', essentially in the back of your mind. When the need arises in another school, especially one that can benefit from that individual's talents, you must ask yourself, 'do you keep them where they are, do you bring them to the new place?'. The key is to balance whether not acting in time will mean they go elsewhere, or prematurely taking them to a new role means they will sink and not swim. Timing is everything to ensure talented individuals will progress and grow with you and won't feel compelled to go elsewhere. Our social professional development events like our Chai & Chat, Leadership Supper, and Jazz Club CPD, are all opportunities where we invite our talent and provide opportunities for rich discussions, as well as identifying whether action is needed.

The Teaching Lead

As is the case with PD leads within many schools, the lead for PD across a trust may also have oversight of teaching and pedagogy as part of their remit; they may work with colleagues across the trust to improve the quality of teaching specifically. Indeed, they may have teaching or pedagogy as part of their job title. However, it is important to note that PD is not just about teaching and learning. Trust PD is about helping teaching *and* non-teaching colleagues get a little bit better in their role every day. As such, while PD and teaching and learning are often synonymous, the leader of PD in a trust may not focus solely on it. Here, Jade Pearce, Director of Professional Development at Greenwood Academies Trust, explains what this means in her trust:

> One of the main aims at Greenwood Academies Trust over the last year has been to develop agreed principles of effective teaching and learning across our 26 primary schools, in order to ensure a shared and consistent understanding of excellent teaching, a common language, a joint and equitable PD offer and consistency in our practice. We were clear that whilst we wanted to improve practice across our schools, it was crucial for schools to retain their autonomy. Therefore, our aim was to develop principles or foundations of effective teaching, as opposed to a more prescriptive approach or list of strategies.

> This has been achieved through a process of collaboration. We have combined the knowledge and experience of our school and trust leaders with extensive reading of research and have jointly developed 'The nine principles of high-quality inclusive teaching at GAT'. This process has been led by our school leaders, with myself and other trust leaders facilitating this through the provision of research materials and discussion points, making refinements and actioning feedback.

This has helped to ensure that our agreed principles are owned by and applicable to all our schools.

Our task was then to implement the teaching and learning principles into our schools. Here, I worked in close collaboration with trust and school leaders to create guidance documents and professional development sessions and materials for both teachers and teaching assistants, along with an online platform to allow for asynchronous professional development. Other trust leaders and I have worked with school leaders to review their current practice, identify priorities and develop implementation plans.

This process is certainly not complete, and our future plans include developing our use of coaching around our teaching and learning principles and to build a trust review process.

Trust professional development: Opportunities and challenges

Opportunities

While the body of literature on the importance of high-quality PD is relatively large, the body of literature on the role trusts have in ensuring this in their schools is much smaller. In 2022, CST published 'Professional development in school trusts: Capacity, conditions and culture' (Barker & Patten, 2022). This paper seeks to set out how trusts can help their schools overcome the barriers associated with delivering high-quality PD. As the title of the paper suggests, the authors conclude that trusts are in a strong position to provide the capacity, create the right conditions and set the right culture to enable high-quality professional learning to happen. These are the opportunities leaders of PD across a trust have.

Capacity

Firstly, turning our attention to providing capacity. Barker and Patten suggest that MATs can provide the capacity (in terms of both expertise and resources) needed for PD to be successful. Individual schools may lack the expertise or resources to enable high-quality PD. However, it is clear from the case studies presented in this chapter that, as fixers, knowers and deliverers, leaders of PD in trusts have an opportunity to overcome these barriers. Whether it is using expertise to deliver high-quality PD, using scale and resources to organise conferences, or knowing who to turn to, internally or externally, for quality PD, we have seen that trust PD leads certainly do have the opportunity to add capacity to enabling PD.

I would add a further type of capacity that trust PD leads can offer: cognitive capacity. School life is incredibly hectic and a source of significant cognitive load. It can be difficult for PD leads in schools to have the space to think either strategically or practically to address PD needs. However, there is an opportunity for trust PD leads, who may not have the extraneous load of managing the day-to-day running of a school, to offer support with that strategic and practical thinking.

Conditions

Next, let's turn our attention to the opportunity trust PD leads have to help set the right conditions to enable high-quality PD. Systems and structures need to be in place to ensure that time and space are given to PD. Barker and Patten suggest that trusts are in a strong position to either directly set those conditions or influence them. We have seen in the case studies in this chapter that as talent mappers and facilitators, trust PD leads can indeed support the establishment of these conditions. For example, this may be through direct coaching of a senior leader in a school to help them to find time and space in their school's timetable for PD to take place, or enabling the conditions for the development of talent in the organisation to be mapped through ITE, ECF, NPQ and so on.

Culture

Finally, Barker and Patten suggest that trusts are in a strong position to help their schools develop the right culture to enable PD to flourish. If PD is not valued or is not seen as worthwhile, then it is unlikely to have the desired impact. We have seen in the case studies in this chapter that trust PD leads do indeed have the ability to help set the right culture. Whether it is working on an improvement project to introduce regular low-stakes lesson visits and valuable next steps or delivering really-high-quality PD that is valued by staff, the trust PD lead can really make a difference.

Challenges

While I have already cited some of the benefits of being part of a MAT as identified in Ofsted's 2019 investigation, the report also highlights a number of challenges. Although the report is not solely focused on PD, many of the general challenges of MAT functioning can be seen as translating directly to trust-wide PD. A trust leader of PD needs to attempt to overcome these challenges.

One of the key challenges identified for schools in a MAT is a potential loss of decision-making. The investigation highlights the tension between individual school autonomy and trust centralisation and consistency. This is a potential challenge for any trust leader, not least for a leader of PD. To what extent should trust PD be consistent in terms of both content and methodology across all schools in the trust? While centralising decision-making may add capacity and influence the conditions and culture for PD, these things are only beneficial if the centralised decision-making is valued by, and relevant to, individual schools.

A second key challenge identified in Ofsted's findings is that while trusts have the potential to enable the sharing of good practice, this is not always done effectively. If a trust PD lead is responsible for facilitating sharing good practice, then they will need to consider how to overcome challenges that may prevent this being done effectively. For example, what is the best way to share best practice if the schools within the trust are geographically dispersed? How do PD leads ring-fence time for sharing best practice if, for example, schools within their trust do not have the same start and finish times or training days? Moreover, while there are logistical challenges to overcome, the more significant challenge is a philosophical one: what if the schools within the trust do not agree with either a) what is being highlighted as best practice and b) what is considered a priority for their school at that time?

A third challenge identified by Ofsted is that, potentially, the larger the organisation, the slower the decision-making process. With more people to consult and update, what could have been a relatively quick decision in a single school can become a much more drawn-out affair in a MAT. This raises two specific challenges for the PD lead. Firstly, PD is more likely to be effective if the goal of the PD is shared by individuals partaking in it. For example, it is more likely for PD on a strategy for managing behaviour to be effective if an individual teacher feels that it is a goal worth personally pursuing (EEF, 2021). One way to achieve that buy-in is for the individual teacher to feel they have contributed to the goal in the first place. This is difficult on an individual school level, and it is even more of a challenge to secure buy-in across multiple schools. The second challenge it raises is more about the outcome of the decision, rather than the decision-making itself. While Barker and Patten suggest that trusts can influence conditions and culture to enable PD to flourish, the extent to which trust leaders can make changes directly to conditions and culture will vary significantly depending on the operating model of the trust. This can mean a PD lead may do all they can to influence change, but it may not occur because such change can only be implemented by school leaders.

Finally, a further challenge cited by Ofsted is that of financial arrangements. MAT central teams are most often funded through a percentage of an individual school's budget being paid to the MAT. In return, the school should expect to enjoy the benefits mentioned earlier in this chapter. Financial arrangements for PD vary from trust to trust: some trusts have a single centralised PD budget that individual schools bid to access for their own uses, whereas other trusts may have a centralised PD budget alongside each individual school having one. Whatever the set-up, questions remain about what any centralised PD budget is spent on and who determines what the money should be prioritised for.

Conclusion

Trusts, like most large organisations, are complex. As we have seen in this chapter, MAT PD leads can have a tricky job to navigate these complexities. However, and I am sure I am not alone in this sentiment, it truly is a privilege to be able to do so. At The Two Counties Trust, each member of staff and each student devises their own legacy sentence – a statement detailing, somewhat morbidly, how we would want to be remembered; in other words, what our personal motivation and purpose is. Mine is simply: 'He helped me to get even better'. It is truly an honour to go to work every day, to support the 1500 staff within my trust to get a little bit better every day so that collectively, we can best serve the 11,000 students across our schools. Hopefully my daughter knows what her daddy does now and is still proud of him!

References

Barker, J. & Patten, K. (2022). 'Professional development in school trusts: Capacity, conditions and culture'. Nottingham: Confederation of School Trusts. Available at: https://cstuk.org.uk/knowledge/guidance-and-policy/policies-professional-development/development-in-school-trusts-capacity-conditions-and-culture/.

BESA. (2021). Key UK education statistics. [online]. Available at: https://www.besa.org.uk/key-uk-education-statistics.

Confederation of School Trusts. (2022). 'What is a strong trust? A CST discussion paper'. Nottingham: Confederation of School Trusts. Available at: https://cstuk.org.uk/knowledge/discussion-and-policy-papers/what-is-a-strong-trust-a-cst-discussion-paper/.

DfE. (2012). 'Attainment at key stage 4 by pupils in academies 2011'. DfE. Available at: https://www.gov.uk/government/publications/attainment-at-key-stage-4-by-pupils-in-academies-2011.

DfE. (2015). 'Policy paper: 2010 to 2015 government policy: academies and free schools'. DfE. Available at: https://www.gov.uk/government/publications/2010-to-2015-government-policy-academies-and-free-schools/2010-to-2015-government-policy-academies-and-free-schools.

DfE. (2022a). 'Opportunity for all: strong schools with great teachers for your child'. Available at: https://assets.publishing.service.gov.uk/media/62416cb5d3bf7f32add7819f/Opportunity_for_all_strong_schools_with_great_teachers_for_your_child__print_version_.pdf.

DfE. (2022b). 'The case for a fully trust-led system'. Available at: https://assets.publishing.service.gov.uk/media/62865295d3bf7f1f433ae170/The_case_for_a_fully_trust-led_system.pdf.

DfE. (2022c). 'Delivering world-class teacher development: Policy paper'. Available at: https://www.gov.uk/government/publications/reforms-to-teacher-development.

EEF. (2021). 'Effective professional development: guidance report'. Education Endowment Foundation.Available at: https://educationendowmentfoundation.org.uk/education-evidence/guidance-reports/effective-professional-development.

Hatton, A., Hampson, R. & Drake, R. (2019). 'An analysis of the performance of sponsored academies: Analytical research report'. Government Statistical Service/DfE. Available at: https://assets.publishing.service.gov.uk/media/5f4fb988d3bf7f610032e834/Sponsored_Academy_Research_Report.pdf.

Haves, E. (2022). 'Education: multi-academy trusts'. UK Parliament/House of Lords Library. Available at: https://lordslibrary.parliament.uk/education-multi-academy-trusts.

House of Commons Education Committee. (2017). 'Multi-academy trusts'. Available at: https://publications.parliament.uk/pa/cm201617/cmselect/cmeduc/204/204.pdf.

Male, T. (2022). 'The rise and rise of academy trusts: continuing changes to the state-funded school system in England'. *School Leadership & Management*, 42(4), pp.313–333.

Ofsted. (2019). 'Multi-academy trusts: benefits, challenges and functions.' Available at: https://assets.publishing.service.gov.uk/media/5fb410838fa8f54ab08176f5/Multi_academy_trusts_benefits_challenges_and_functions.pdf.

Webber, E. (2016). *Building Successful Communities of Practice: Discover How Connecting People Makes Better Organisations*. San Francisco: Blurb.